Winning Words

Winning Words

Devotions for Athletes

Curtis French

WORD BOOKS
PUBLISHER
WACO, TEXAS

A DIVISION OF
WORD, INCORPORATED

WINNING WORDS

Scripture quotations are from the *King James Version*
of the Bible.

ISBN: 0-8499-2805-2
Library of Congress catalog card number: 77-075467
Printed in the United States of America

First Printing, October 1977
Second Printing, November 1977
Third Printing, July 1978
Fourth Printing, April 1983

To the Christ who dwells within every Christian athlete
To Coach Bill Yung, a Christian
To my wife, Kathy, who first saw the real worth of this material

Contents

Foreword

I believe in the three-dimensional athlete. As coaches and athletes, we spend much time in the mental and physical preparation for our athletic goals, but I believe spiritual growth and development is as vital as the other two.

Everything that goes into our minds becomes a part of us. Daily Bible study, prayer, and devotion are just as important as weight training, agility, drills, and conditioning work.

Winning Words allows you to correlate those things which are spiritual and those things which are athletic. It is a perfect personal devotional book and great for sharing with others.

May God bless you as you continue to grow as a three-dimensional athlete.

GRANT TEAFF
Head Football Coach
Baylor University

Preface

Sports, whether it be vocation or avocation, has produced its own vocabulary. Athletes in conversation with each other or commentators giving the play-by-play use words whose meanings are particularly identified with the sporting event being described. Such sports terms are often carried over into other realms of society. Thus other people who aren't even remotely involved in active sports may use such words in their daily conversation.

It is interesting to note that many athletic words are found in Scripture. Often these athletic terms in Scripture are used in very much the same way as today, while others have quite different usages.

An athlete may be inspired by the greatness of another. Inspiration may also come from a tremendous desire to excel. Many of today's athletes, through the encouragement of their churches, or a particular team or campus ministry have performed mightily with a mission far beyond that which takes place in the arena of sports competition. Theirs is an inspiration from within, produced by a character and stamina only available from a Power beyond their capabilities. To identify that Power is simply to say, Immanuel "God with us." That was the name given to Jesus Christ and it is Christ's name that now is identified more and more in today's truly great athlete.

Winning Words is an attempt to encourage athletes to look into the Scriptures. In the Scriptures there is God; His only begotten Son, Jesus; and the quickening and renewing Holy Spirit. God gives His Word as a channel for developing faith in us. "Faith cometh by hearing, and hearing by the Word of God" (Rom. 10:17).

Sports words, and all other words, in the Bible are truly *Winning Words*. Read them. Receive them. Be a winner!

CURTIS FRENCH

1. Attain

1.

Attain

Such knowledge is too wonderful for me; it is high, I cannot attain unto it.

—Psalm 139:6

Achievements in life generally come only to those who set goals for themselves. We only *attain* that which we set our sights on. I suppose that's the difference between a friendly game on the vacant lot and a conference game on a Friday or Saturday before thousands of people. Winning brings satisfaction, whether on the vacant lot or in the packed stadium. However, what is attained in both instances is quite different. The higher the goal, the greater the satisfaction in attaining it. A team which has become a winner has done so by certain individuals setting and reaching goals for themselves.

Some people look upon life as just a friendly game on a vacant lot. Nothing lost, and very little gained. Life is going nowhere because there's nowhere to go. Just play the game, take your licks, and if there's anything out there, you're bound to stumble on to a piece of it.

Maybe it's time we looked up to see where we're going. Yes, there are goals in life just as there are paydays and congratulations. No goals in life? Then why are there goal posts and goal lines; backboards and baskets; tapes and finishes; homeplates and home runs; pins, points, and pucks; victories and defeats? All are part of the pursuit called attaining. The great Apostle Paul said in Philippians 3:11, "If by any means I might *attain* unto the resurrection of the dead." That's exactly what life is without attainment . . . dead! Christ wants to bring us to life. He said, "I am come that they might have life, and that they might have it more abundantly" (John 10:10). The Apostle Paul also said, "I press toward the mark for the prize of the high calling of God in Christ Jesus" (Phil. 3:14).

As you set your sights on Jesus, put your life in his hands. With Christ at the controls, goals and attainments are promised. "I can do all things through Christ which strengtheneth me" (Phil. 4:13).

Prayer
Heavenly Father, I realize the pursuit of earthly goals is a part of your plan to condition in me a desire for heavenly attainments far beyond my reach. May I never settle for less than your highest for my life.

2.

Balance

A just weight and balance are the Lord's.

—Proverbs 16:11

Balance is a desired quality from two standpoints. First, the athlete who can play his position in complete control of his body and reflexes is free to perform with all his capabilities. The runner, the shooter, or the thrower who is kept off *balance* will experience a great deal of anguish and frustration as he tries to compete. *Balance* is essential to the individual athlete.

Second, *balance* is a trait which coaches try to achieve with their teams. A balanced team is one which does not depend too heavily upon one or two individual performers. Balanced teams are more difficult to defense. Coaches strive for a *balance* between offense and defense so that extra pressure need not be experienced by those trying to score or those defending.

Life is, without a doubt, most difficult to *balance*. It is so easy for us to find that which is easiest and most convenient and plot our lives in that direction. A person who "goes with the flow" in respect to life will find himself all out of *balance*, sometimes before he realizes it.

In order for our lives to *balance*, there must be a just

17

weight on the other side. We need a standard against which to weigh our lives. Compared to Christ, our weights just don't stack up! In order to *balance*, a proper and just weight is essential.

Sometimes we think our lives *balance* just by looking around at what others are doing. We *balance* just fine when compared to the world's mad rush and preoccupation with sex and material things. You may have said, "Now how am I ever going to balance out in God's standard?" His standard is high, to be sure! Perfection, no less. Have we considered this? Jesus Christ is the only person who can meet God's standard. Only he can *balance* equally with God. The only way our lives will ever approach God's standard is to accept Christ into our lives. With God as the just weight and Christ as the *balance*, our lives can have the purpose God initially intended.

Christ is alive today in the hearts of the redeemed. "To [you] whom God would make known what is the riches of the glory of this mystery . . . which is Christ in you, the hope of glory" (Col. 1:27).

Prayer
Father in heaven, I realize today that only Christ can give my life the balance needed to be approved by you.

3.

Banner

Thou hast given a banner to them that fear thee, that it may be displayed because of the truth.

—Psalm 60:4

The champion is presented a *banner*. It is displayed in a place where all may observe and bask in the glory of the achievement it represents. It is hoped that banners will inspire others to higher achievement and create a sense of pride in the school and campus. "Our team is the best, so I want to be the best." The truth and claims of the *banner* will hang unchallenged until the next season when it must be proven again. The *banner* that waves continually over the same place indicates that many challenges have been pushed back.

The type of *banner* identifies the sport or conference represented. Symbols and words spell out the facts that exalt the winner. In the beautiful imagery of Song of Solomon, God's *banner* is described as love. "He brought me to the banqueting house, and his banner over me was love" (Song of Sol. 2:4). God's *banner* identifies him. God is love, and every act he extends toward man is out of a heart of love and a desire for man's ultimate good and betterment. As usual, many challenges have been made toward the supremacy of his love, but God has withstood them all. "Greater love hath

19

no man than this" (John 15:13). "I have loved thee with an everlasting love" (Jer. 31:3). "And to know the love of Christ which passeth knowledge . . ." (Eph. 3:19). God's love has no rival. It is unsurpassed!

With Christ living in our lives, this is our *banner* too. Wouldn't it be wonderful if all human relations were based on love? Of course, this is only possible through Christ. "For God so loved the world that he gave his only begotten Son that whosoever believeth in him should not perish, but have everlasting life" (John 3:16). With Christ in your life, every year is a *banner* year!

Prayer
Dear Lord, love through me today as I carry the Christian banner before all who observe my life.

4.

Body

But I keep under my body, and bring it into subjection.
                                             —1 Corinthians 9:27

A strong and healthy *body* is of vital importance to an athlete. Injuries are of such constant concern to coaches that precautionary measures are frequently taken. Exercising, training, and the proper rest and diet are all a part of a coach's responsibility in developing outstanding players. In short, the athlete usually performs no better than the condition of his *body* allows. Young aspiring athletes should heed carefully the advice of coaches in keeping their bodies physically qualified for competition. This usually requires the curtailing of certain activities so that energies are not expended on less worthwhile things. The athlete who is not willing to train and bring his *body* into shape will not make a significant contribution to the team.

We must realize also that our bodies express what we are, morally and spiritually. We are outwardly demonstrating what there is on the inside. Billy Graham once said, "America is demonstrating that our emphasis is mostly on the outside, not inside." Some people who profess to be good and kind are betrayed by the activity of their bodies. Consequently, the Apostle Paul says, "I bring my body into subjection." The athlete is motivated to keep his *body* strong and healthy by the competition which he faces and the demands made upon his *body*. A Christian athlete has even deeper motivation. The moment we open our mouths, in defense of morality and the ministry of Jesus Christ, people are going to begin to watch our bodies. Our bodies must reflect the principles which come forth in our confessions. This is only accomplished by allowing Christ to be in control. God wants "living sacrifices" (Rom. 12:1), not simply the left-overs of previous indulgences!

Your *body* in good condition is important to your coach and team, but it's vitally more important to Jesus Christ. Through our bodies Christ wants to show the world his capabilities in creating the best life for men. Presenting your *body* to Christ will certainly not lessen your contribution to the team. To the contrary, in Christ, we realize potential we never knew was there before.

Prayer
Lord Jesus, my body is your earthly dwelling place. I yield my body today to be subject to your wishes.

5.

Call

Call unto me, and I will answer thee, and shew thee great and mighty things which thou knowest not.

—Jeremiah 33:3

As important as fundamentals and execution are in a game situation, the results often depend on the right *call* in the right situation. The *call* may be a play selection, defensive alignment, individual maneuver, or a sign from the catcher to the pitcher. The action immediately following the *call* may spark debate as to whether or not it was the proper one. The next play after the *call* has often turned out to be an interception, a decisive basket, or a long home run that sailed into the upper deck. On the positive side, the right *call* has often resulted in victory: a touchdown pass, a blocked shot, or the umpire's authoritative cry, "Strike three, you're out of there!"

Although the *call* may be made quickly, a lot goes into it. Many questions have to be instantly asked and answered relative to the situation and personnel—hopefully resulting in the statement, "good *call!*"

Today our Scripture from Jeremiah indicates man's best *call*. A *call* and an answer from God opens a resource beyond man's capabilities. God is not apprehensive about the results

23

of your *call*. He says, "I will answer thee and shew thee. . . ." As sure as there are results from an athletic *call*, God promises and answers when we call on him. God is even careful to say that the result of our *call* will be "great and mighty things which thou knowest not." A *call* to God is not a good luck charm, it is an admission of some area which we don't know. It is also a demonstration of our confidence in God's ability to deliver. People who never *call* on God obviously do not believe there is valid reason to do so.

Our best *call* today, regardless of our situation, is to request resources beyond our own from God. "If any of you lack wisdom, let him ask of God, that giveth to all men liberally . . ." (James 1:5).

If your soul is lost and you've never established contact with your Savior, he's still your best call. "Whosoever shall call upon the name of the Lord shall be saved" (Rom. 10:13).

Prayer
Father, teach me that my best call is a call and an answer from you.

6.
Choice

. . . *He chose of all the choice men of Israel, and put them in array against the Syrians.*

—2 Samuel 10:9

Prior to the beginning of each season of competition, sportswriters select the *choice* teams in the order of their predicted finish. Though the selection of the top team may vary, usually the *choice* teams are generally agreed upon. *Choice* teams are composed of *choice* men, not only men of ability, but also men of proven quality in the battle. Every coach would prefer to begin each season with experienced players who have some battle time. To be the *choice* team is quite an honor, but the truth of the selection still must be proven in the contest.

In the Scripture today, Joab was the one making the choices. God is seeking out *choice* persons also. God's team is an eternal winner because he makes no mistakes in his selections. Being on God's squad doesn't begin with us, for God makes the choices. Matthew 20:16 indicates that many may be called Christians but few are actually chosen by God. There are more qualifications than just going around with a Jesus sticker on our cars or coats. Celebration is wonderful, but it should always follow the battle. The people on God's team are chosen by him because of their desire to be in the

25

battle (1 Pet. 2:9). God has a way of knowing those of us who've really, sincerely chosen him. The test is in the battle, not in the cheering section, not in the headlines, not in the coaching staff. Has God counted you worthy to be in the battle?

Maybe all you lack is just a simple commitment of your life. It could be the confession (agreeing with God) of some sin in your life that keeps you from qualifying. Remember the words of Jesus in John 15:16, "Ye have not chosen me, but I have chosen you, and ordained you, that ye should go and bring forth fruit." To be the *choice* of God—that's the ultimate recognition. That's life's highest goal!

Prayer
Lord, I want to offer myself for the battle today. May I never be satisfied to stand on the sidelines in the game of life.

7.

Conversion

. . . The law of the Lord is perfect, converting the soul.

—Psalm 19:7

Sometimes the most decisive play in a game is when a *conversion* takes place. A football team has just tied the score with a touchdown; a *conversion* will put them ahead. A basketball player has just made a basket and was fouled in the process; the free throw will convert his field goal into more points for the team. By a successful *conversion*, the score was changed.

According to the Bible, the score of our lives is not high enough to be on the winning side when the final whistle is blown. We've inherited the team colors of Adam who sinned and was driven out of his beautiful garden by God. Our soul is in a losing struggle with the clock; *conversion* must take place before time runs out. As with an athletic *conversion*, certain rules must be observed before a soul *conversion* takes place and is counted as valid. The *conversion* of the soul from eternal condemnation to eternal life takes place when we believe on the Lord Jesus Christ. The law of the Lord for spiritual *conversion:* "Whosoever shall call upon the name of the Lord shall be saved" (Rom. 10:13).

27

Prayer

Dear Savior, today I repent of my sin and selfish life. I turn to you for forgiveness. I want to be God's child so I call upon you.

8.

Deal

. . . They that deal truly are his delight
— Proverbs 12:22

Whether formal or informal, a *deal* is said to be a transaction between men. "We made a *deal*" or "a deal is a *deal*" are statements often made as a reminder of a gentlemen's agreement. I suppose the word derives much of its meaning from card games in which a dealer shuffles the deck and distributes cards for the players. A dealer may also be the local merchant who sells his wares to the public.

In sports much dealing is done between owners of professional teams in trading or buying a ball player's services. Sportswriters often refer to trades which either proved to be a help or a hindrance to the teams involved. Owners and managers evaluate personnel and study deals that could help strengthen their team.

High school and college athletes know the meaning of the word also. Terms upon which a high school athlete is recruited may be described as "a good *deal*." College athletes talk of the *deal* they were offered to sign a professional contract.

Unfortunately, all transactions between men are not honest and aboveboard. Quite often we may hear of someone complaining about getting "the short end of the *deal*." He made a *deal* which he thought was to his advantage, only to find the other party came out ahead. A *deal* that profits both parties equally seems to be a rare thing.

There is one who deals with us who is described as "faithful and just" (1 John 1:9), "rich in mercy" (Eph. 2:4), and "excellent in lovingkindness" (Ps. 36:7). God wants us to be obedient children. He delights in those who *"deal* truly," that is, those who are honest with him about themselves. One who is honest with himself must *deal* truly and honestly with others. In Hebrews 12, God speaks of how he disciplines his children. Verse seven says, "If ye endure chastening, God dealeth with you as with sons . . . ." God's desire is to be our father and for us to respond as sons.

Before such a relationship is possible, God has his initial *deal*. We must acknowledge Jesus Christ as his Son and accept his sacrifice for our sin on Calvary's cross. We must do something about our sin. We'll either suffer for it in eternity or we'll accept Christ's death as sacrifice for our sin. God said through John, "If we say that we have no sin, we deceive ourselves, and the truth is not in us" (1 John 1:8). What will you do about it? You can become one with whom God deals as a son. "But as many as received him, to them gave he power to become the sons of God . . ." (John 1:12). That's the best *deal* going!

Prayer
Father in heaven, I am grateful to be dealt with as your child. Lead me as a loving father leads his son.

2. Balance

9.

Defeat

. . . As I have been thy father's servant hitherto, so will I now also be thy servant: then mayest thou for me defeat the counsel of Ahithophel.

—2 Samuel 15:34

Defeat! It's a word and an experience that we want to know only from the positive side. We enjoy administering *defeat,* but we sorely dislike having it happen to us. Every contest is intended to produce a winner and a loser. It is often said that more lessons are learned in *defeat* than in victory. That's only true if we profit from our losses. *Defeat* is only temporary for the coach and team who can strengthen weaknesses that showed up in a losing effort. The most dangerous of all effects of *defeat* is to accept it as proof of inferiority. In an attitude of accepting defeat, the possibility of winning is so remote that no one really expects it. Many so-called "upsets" are not really that at all, because the underdog who believes he can win will play with expectation.

Defeat in the spiritual realm is one of Satan's most effective tools. The Christian who is spiritually whipped can either learn from his weaknesses or become a loser. Some people seem to receive a measure of contentment just in being able to explain their losses. "The devil made me do it," they say.

That's all the explanation they seem to need. The devil only takes what we offer him. The team that goes out on the field and simply lies down and is overrun is a disgrace to everyone involved—yet so many times this is our tactic against Satan.

Life is going to have its mixture of victories and defeats. Just as victories are not to puff us up, defeats should not flatten us out! Our strength in *defeat* is in Christ! Our triumph over Satan is in Christ! There were times even when our Lord faced certain *defeat*, but he always came out victorious. Jesus said, "These things have I spoken unto you, that in me ye might have peace. In the world ye shall have tribulation [defeat]: but be of good cheer; I have overcome the world" (John 16:33).

Prayer
Lord Jesus, I do not want to be a loser. By your power, make life's defeats steps toward ultimate triumph.

10.

Early

. . . those that seek me early shall find me.
—Proverbs 8:17

The team that can mount a big lead *early* in the game can usually control the game the rest of the way. Opportunistic teams capitalize on the opposition's mistakes and jump to an *early* lead. *Early* leads have proven many times to be the turning points in games. A coach may lament after the game, "We just got too far behind *early* in the game." However, many teams have watched almost helplessly as an *early* lead dwindled away to a narrow victory or even a loss.

Most positions on the team are nailed down *early* in the season. Coaches like to solidify their line-up as *early* in the season as possible. Aspiring ballplayers go out and prove themselves *early* so that they can become a part of the coach's plans for the season ahead. Showing up for practice early and getting in extra work always makes a good impression.

Statistics tell us that it is wise to open our lives to God *early* in life. After a person reaches age twenty-five, according to figures, his chances for becoming a Christian decrease drastically. It isn't that God can't save a person past twenty-five, it is simply that as the years pass by, we become more concerned with other pursuits of life. The person who allows

35

his mind and life to be cluttered will give less thought to his eternal destiny. Our text today states, "Those that seek me early shall find me." In Ecclesiastics 12:1 we are urged, "Remember now thy Creator in the days of thy youth, while the evil days come not, nor the years draw nigh, when thou shalt say, I have no pleasure in them."

The Apostle John gave his life to Christ in his late teens. He was the youngest of the disciples, yet he was the only one of all the disciples who stood at the foot of the cross as Jesus Christ was being crucified. It was the greatest moment of crisis in Jesus' life and in the lives of his disciples, yet John stood firm in the crisis.

As a young athlete, give your life to Christ. His power and blessing on your life and your influence for Him will double every experience you have ahead of you. "And the world passeth away, and the lust thereof: but he that doeth the will of God abideth for ever" (1 John 2:17). "O God, thou art my God; early will I seek thee: my soul thirsteth for thee" (Ps. 63:1).

Prayer
Lord, I come to you giving my whole life for your use, while my life and body are young and strong. Fill my early years with divine strength and power for the crisis to come.

11.

Endure

Can thine heart endure, or can thine hands be strong, in the days that I shall deal with thee?

—Ezekiel 22:14

In every sport there are moments which test a player's endurance. To be fresh and strong in the early moments of a contest is quite normal and to be expected. Just the excitement of competition produces momentary stamina that serves the athlete well in the initial stages. But when the game wears on—in the last quarter, or you're rounding the turn for the last lap of the race—maybe you've already made several trips around the bases or up and down the court, is there anything left to draw upon? Endurance requires that you continue to function and be alert, to set aside the fatigue and weariness of your body. "The game is not over until the last whistle is blown," is a quotation we've heard many times. How true it is!

Though endurance is an athletic quality dependent upon the condition of the heart, we are not necessarily born with it. A great athlete may not naturally possess the character to *endure*. Endurance is a result of a decision made from within. The other team is passing; your body is tired! You must con-

37

tinue to exercise good judgment and maintain control of your body.

The word *endure* carries with it a feeling of longsuffering, withstanding over a period of time something demanding or perhaps distasteful. Paul wrote to Timothy (2 Tim. 2:3), "Thou therefore endure hardness, as a good soldier of Jesus Christ." Christians who endure are not simply those who smile and say, "Everything's all right." To *endure* is to hurt! If you're not hurting, what is there to *endure?*

Your contribution to the team ought to cost you some hurting! Your position as a Christian among unredeemed people requires endurance. Simply smiling and laughing off our problems is not endurance. Common sense tells us that when we hurt is when we are most prone to action.

Christ hurt for sinners—for sorrowing people, for a city, for disobedient disciples, and for sick people. But he "endured the cross" (Heb. 12:2) for every person who will come to him. Can your heart *endure?*

Prayer
God, I realize that to be like Christ requires some hurting and endurance. May I receive what comes to me today in the spirit of your will for me.

12.
Fail

. . . O Lord: my spirit faileth: hide not thy face from me. . . .

—Psalm 143:7

One of life's greatest fears is failure. Some people never participate in competitive sports for the simple reason they don't want to *fail*. "Nothing ventured, nothing failed" would be their interpretation of an old saying. This fear of failure is more than just a lack of confidence. It is a preoccupation with self-image designed to minimize experiences of defeat.

Athletics, in order to provide lessons in life, must always be accompanied by the possibility of failure and defeat. To *fail* in athletics is to realize an area of weakness, not to succumb to it. It appears at times as though some people are looking for a reason to quit! Upon noticing a glaring weakness and experiencing failure, an athlete may just "check out" of the situation and leave it alone forever. It seems so easy to forsake a real test, but a pattern of response could be developed that would prove very unfulfilling throughout life. I believe all failures must be looked upon as challenges to overcome. However, I realize that some weaknesses are inherent. For these so-called "explainable failures," we all have strengths that can be used to compensate. For every inherent

39

weakness, there is a corresponding strength. Infielders whose arms weren't necessarily strong have compensated with a quick release of the ball or greater use of their bodies. The pitcher who can't throw the "smoker" compensates by changing speeds and keeping the batter off-stride.

An athlete must be free to *fail,* or else he will never take the field and compete. Some people on occasion say, "I'm not going to try to be a Christian because I can't live it." It's much easier to follow the natural processes of life and avoid the encounter with Christ. Jesus knew we couldn't live the Christian life. He knew we would *fail!* He came to give us victory beyond ourselves. Jesus is not so much concerned with what our lives are as he is with what we are becoming. "But as many as received him, to them gave he power to become the sons of God" (John 1:12). When you fail in your Christian life, don't quit! Just thank God he has revealed another weakness in your life that you must turn over to his power. As areas of weakness are turned over to Christ for power and control, we are becoming what God wants us to be.

"But I have prayed for thee, that thy faith fail not . . ." (Luke 22:32).

Prayer
Dear Lord, thrust me out today in a venture of faith. Teach me that the possibility of failure is an opportunity for you to reward the faith of your redeemed children.

13.

Forward

But they hearkened not, nor inclined their ear, but walked in the counsels and in the imagination of their evil heart, and went backward, and not forward.

—Jeremiah 7:24

To move *forward*, that's the idea. To improve your game, to increase the score, and to add another win to the column. A few years back Chrysler Corporation increased its sales of cars by quite a percentage with a theme called, "The Forward Look." The idea caught on because people like to be found moving *forward*.

Moving *forward* is not simply a matter of doing. It also requires much listening. Coaches know that the athlete who is coachable must listen well to instruction. Only by listening and mastering the fundamentals can an athlete ever become his own man. The moment he stops listening, the athlete is apt to go backward, not *forward*.

A parallel is easily drawn here in the spiritual realm. God intends for us to keep learning, listening, and growing. Often we have all experienced periods of rapid growth and deepening in our spiritual lives. What a joy it is to be moving *forward* in our life in Christ. We hunger for the Word of God, for the fellowship of other Christians, and God has given us

41

a sense of purpose in our lives. Then it happens. We gradually begin operating in our own strength, and we listen to God with less attention than before. Before we know it our lives, that were moving *forward* in Christ, have now taken a backward turn. Instead of consulting God, our lives take on a do-it-yourself character.

No other *forward* step in business or in influence must supersede our growth in Christ. The psalmist said, "God set my feet upon a rock and established my goings."

What step *forward* in Christ is needed for you at this moment? If God has ordained it, to restrain yourself would constitute a step backward. Forward—in and through Jesus Christ.

Prayer
Father in heaven, I come now submitting myself to go forward and deeper in my relationship with you. Let your spirit guard me from slipping backward.

14.

Gap

And I sought for a man among them, that should make up the hedge, and stand in the gap before me for the land. . . .
—Ezekiel 22:30

An opening in our defense makes us vulnerable to the attack of the opposition. Coaches and players whose responsibility is defense work hard and long to eliminate gaps in their coverage. The whole theory behind the position of linebacker in football is to fill in gaps created by the maneuvers of the defensive linemen. A familiar phrase heard by linebackers for years is "you move over and fill in the *gap* . . . ." A wise quarterback or playmaker can spot a *gap* in the defense. If that *gap* is not filled during the ensuing play, valuable yards and even points lost could be the result. A special kind of person is needed to stand alone in the *gap* against an oncoming blocker and ball carrier. Though he is just one man, he seldom sees only one coming into his area of protection.

Sometimes an injury or other misfortune creates a *gap* in an otherwise experienced and formidable defense. Someone has to step in. That man is invariably compared to his predecessor, so he's on the spot immediately. Sports history is

43

replete with stories of players who have "filled the *gap*" and performed admirably as replacements.

Our Scripture for today indicates that God has some openings for those ready to stand in the *gap* for him. God wants representation on your *team!* He wants athletes who will stand for him. Christian athletes! That term has gained great respect throughout the world in recent years, primarily because of the kind of people involved.

Jesus is a man in the *gap*. Because of sin, there is a "great gulf fixed" (Luke 16:26) between us and God. Christ is the link that joins man with God. Because of the tremendous qualifications necessary, Jesus Christ was the only possible mediator in the *gap* between man and God. He made it possible for you and I to know God personally and communicate with him through prayer and the Word.

Jesus has opened the way to God for you. "I am the way, the truth, and the life: no man cometh unto the Father, but by me" (John 14:6).

Prayer
Jesus, thank you for standing in the gap for me before God the Father. Use me to bridge the gap in others' lives whom you want to touch.

15.

Gift

Thanks be unto God for his unspeakable gift.
—2 Corinthians 9:15

Most teams would rather win a hard-fought victory than win on *gift* points. Matching strengths, wits, and proficiency and coming away with a victory is much more satisfying than winning against an outclassed opponent. Losing teams certainly don't enjoy giving games away. The one exception may be in a championship game when winning by any means crowns a champion. *Gift* points in crucial situations have made many a coach rest easier.

Unlike the use of the word in other instances, *gift* points come quite unintentionally and not as tokens of good will. In fact, every team and coach would like to have them back.

God's gifts are all intended for the blessing and welfare of his children. "Every good gift and every perfect gift is from above, and cometh down from the Father of lights . . ." (James 1:17). God's gifts are for our good and our perfecting. As God's children we can rightfully thank him for every situation of life.

God's greatest *gift,* indescribable in words is his son, Jesus Christ. Christ is God's contact with men on this earth. Without Christ, all of God's gifts would be unavailable. What a

45

gift! Christ created (John 1:3), gives life (John 10:10), sustains (Col. 1:17), saves (Rom. 10:13), and is preparing a place for us (John 14:23). God loved the world so much that he gave us Jesus (John 3:16)!

God continues his gifts to us in the person of the Holy Spirit. *Holy Spirit* literally means God's life in us. We are God's temple here on this earth, as stated by Paul in 1 Corinthians 6:19. God continues to give us his very life, thus producing power and resources beyond man's capabilities. "If ye then, being evil, know how to give good gifts unto your children: how much more shall your heavenly Father give the Holy Spirit to them that ask him?" (Luke 11:13).

God's gifts are intentional, with all good will, for our good and perfecting. *Indescribable!*

Prayer
Loving Father, my thanks seem so inadequate for your indescribable gift, Jesus Christ. So I give you again a commitment of my life for your divine use.

16.

Halt

. . . All my familiars watched for my halting, saying, "Per-adventure he will be enticed, and we shall prevail against him.
—Jeremiah 20:10

Halt is a word that applies to defense. *Halt* is an answer to a threat by the opposition to take control of the contest. The use of the word implies that someone is trespassing on another's territory. *"Halt!* Who goes there?" has been spoken by soldiers on guard-duty for decades.

Athletic teams are constantly faced with the challenge of halting a threat by the opposition. Two teams seldom run roughshod over each other. Usually one is halted, resulting in victory for the other.

Halt is basically a word denoting action. It actually means "arrested action." Someone or something was moving progressively before being halted. One use of the word means "a prolonged pause." To *halt* is not to terminate completely— this gives the word more of a meaning of hesitation. Such a use of the word is found in 1 Kings 18:21, "And Elijah came unto all the people and said, 'How long halt ye between two opinions?'" God was about to demonstrate his power through Elijah before the people and the prophets of Baal. "When are you going to decide?" was Elijah's question.

The people were hesitating between a decision to follow Baal or Jehovah God. Their loyalty to either had been brought to a *halt* because of their indecision. Elijah was committing himself to prove God's superiority and challenging the people to make a choice. Baal was a man-made God, contrived of man's sensual desires. Those who would follow Baal were simply those who submitted to their own selfish and fleshly lusts. Jehovah is the God of the universe whose desire is to lift man above his own capabilities. Jehovah is the God who would later send his son Jesus Christ to earth to redeem man from sin and self.

Today, it's the same issue! Are we going to follow the God who created us, or one which we've created for ourselves? Man's gods are all like man himself—unpredictable, temperamental, temporal, and unfulfilling. God is everlasting and his son Jesus is the "same yesterday, and to-day, and for ever" (Heb. 13:8).

While you are in the process of choosing, your spiritual life is at a *halt*. ". . . Choose you this day whom ye will serve . . . as for me and my house, we will serve the Lord" (Josh. 24:15).

Prayer
Lord Jesus, I'm grateful that faith in you constantly challenges our priorities. Lead me always to take a stand and to walk in the direction which leads toward you.

7. Conversion

17.

Hands

I will therefore that men pray everywhere, lifting up holy hands, without wrath and doubting.

—1 Timothy 2:8

"He's got good *hands*." The person speaking may have been referring to a young athlete with great pass-catching ability. Or the statement may have been directed toward a slick-fielding shortstop or a sure-handed rebounder. The *hands* of an athlete are a vital part of the tools of his trade. Besides catching and throwing, *hands* are used for balance, for starting, for swinging, for protection, and for encouragement. (If you do your job well, the people in the bleachers may give you a *hand*.) We've all been encouraged at one time or another by a swat on the backside accompanied with the words, "Let's go."

It's an old saying "You can tell a lot about a man by looking at his *hands*." Often our *hands* bear the marks of fierce combat on the field of competition.

What we do with our *hands* is a very definite reflection of our spiritual condition also. If our *hands* are not restrained and brought under divine control, they simply become tools for getting what we want. *Hands* speak measures about a

51

young man's intentions on a date. *Hands* may show either respect or disrespect, honor or disregard.

God is vitally interested in the *hands* of his people. God spoke through the Apostle Paul and said, "Lifting up holy hands." Holy *hands* must be placed under divine discipline. As with the athlete, holy *hands* may bear the marks of the price paid for our redemption.

God doesn't require a kindergarten morning inspection to know if our *hands* are clean or not. No other outside limb of our body is more indicative of our attitude toward God. Does God ever see our *hands* folded in prayer? Does he ever see our *hands* enfolding the Word of God as we read it? Does God ever find our *hands* clasping those of a brother in need?

God once inquired of Moses, "What is that in thine hand?" It was only a simple rod, but Moses turned it over to God, and it became God's rod.

Let your *hands* be a channel through which God works.

Prayer
Father, today and forever, let my hands reveal Christ's redeeming love. Through your guidance, restrain my hands from foolish gestures and selfish pursuits.

18.

Increase

And the word of God increased; and the number of the disciples multiplied.

—Acts 6:7

In a see-saw game, neither team has a chance to *increase* its lead. A game where the lead often changes hands may be a delight to the fans, but it is nerve-wracking to the team and coaches. There isn't much security in simply taking the lead by a slim margin. Once a lead is secured, it is hoped opportunity will come for the lead to be increased. As the lead is increased, the regulars will be rested and more players will get into the game, gaining precious experience for games and years ahead.

The team who ends the season convincingly superior is one who wins by wide margins obviously in control of each game. Coaches seldom purposely run up the score, but increases on the scoreboard serve to insure the victory. Increases on the scoreboard also indicate an *increase* in the proficiency with which the team plays. To improve each week and execute more efficiently is the goal of every team.

Our Christian lives are also subject to *increase*. With every growth experience, God increases our depth of commitment to him. We become more assured of his power and sufficiency through prayer and confirmation of his word. John the Baptist had the key to unlocking life's greatest treasure when he said, "He [Jesus] must increase, but I must decrease" (John 3:30). As Jesus increases in our lives, our lives take on an abundance that was promised by Jesus in coming into the world.

Even Jesus himself is said to have increased as he entered his teen years. Luke 2:52 indicates that "Jesus increased in wisdom and stature, and in favor with God and man." That's quite a commentary on life! I see two major ingredients that could have contributed to Jesus' *increase* in all these areas. First, verse forty-nine says, he was about his heavenly Father's business. Even though his parents didn't understand his mission entirely, Jesus was faithful to it. Second, verse fifty-one shows Jesus was "subject unto them," meaning his earthly parents Mary and Joseph. This is a marvelous example for the Son of God to leave for us!

"He will bless them that fear the Lord, *both* small and great. The Lord will *increase* you more and more, you and your children. Ye are blessed of the Lord which made heaven and earth" (Ps. 115:13–15).

Prayer
Lord, increase the breadth and depth of my life through the study of your word and by serving in your kingdom.

19.

Idol

. . . And how ye turned to God from idols to serve the living and true God.

—1 Thessalonians 1:9

Hero worship has long been associated with athletes. I still remember names of people from my childhood who I held in high esteem for their achievements and recognition. Our *idol* influences our styles of play, our positions, and even the numbers we hope to wear on our uniforms. In the eyes of an admiring fan, the *idol* can do no wrong. Great athletes have been known to attract fan clubs with members numbering in the hundreds.

It is unfortunate that many heros are not aware of their responsibility to those who look up to them. One well-known NFL quarterback has flatly denied via national TV that he has any responsibility to the youth of America.

The dictionary defines an *idol* as "any object of ardent or excessive devotion or admiration." Actually the Bible encourages us to guard against allowing ourselves to develop worshipful attitudes toward other humans. Regardless of personal attainments, any human is just that—a human being, prone to human misjudgment and failures. There is more to the life of our heros than what we see in competition or other public life. The part which we idolize is only an image of the total person. One great athlete relates how much he was enjoying being idolized until he found out what an idol was. He was told by one of his friends that an *idol* is simply a replica, a smaller model of the real thing.

The person who genuinely wants to be a positive influence for good will be real. Regardless of his prowess, he can still be real in all of his relationships. Real people are those who see themselves for what they really are.

Jesus Christ is the only man of all time worthy of our worship. Why? He was the God-man, God in the flesh. He came to earth to release men from false pride and false power so that he could be himself in them. Man was created to be God's temple, and man will never be real until he invites Jesus Christ in.

Are you looking for a hero? Look at Jesus! But more than looking for a pattern, let him be your life (1 John 4:4).

Prayer
Heavenly Father, lead me day by day to turn from idols unto you. Also let me see your son, Jesus, as lord and master and life itself, and not merely idolize him.

20.

Jealousy

For jealousy is the rage of a man.

—Proverbs 6:34

The attitudes of team members toward each other is an important factor in team spirit. The goal of the team is to play together and win. Losing teams can often be explained by attitudes of *jealousy* between team members. A team cannot possibly pull together when there are members who are jealous of each other's success. Team sports are designed to pool the resources of several people toward a common cause. The common good of the team and each of its members ought to prevail above any other attitude. *Jealousy* on the team among one or several of the players deprives the team of the unity necessary to pull together and celebrate the victory equally.

Jealousy and a breach in team spirit usually come when a player puts his own individual performance ahead of the team's collective success. The rest of the team may begin to feel that they are simply contributing to the reputation of the star. Regardless of how great an athlete is, a part of his success is dependent upon the team attitude of his mates. Players who fail to realize this are often victimized as the rest of the team withdraws and allows the star to try and make it on his own. Obviously the total team effort suffers, and success is a remote possibility. Both the star and the rest of the team are now playing as individuals. Not only the team, but the object of team sports has been defeated. Often coaches are called upon to take drastic action in the face of such a situation.

Often different players excel in different aspects of the game. Coaches usually try to field the best combination of strength and weakness. A complete ballplayer, one who is strong in all aspects of the game is not always the rule of thumb, even in professional sports. Players who realize each other's strengths and weaknesses can work together to present a united effort. Each player complements the other. No player should feel more important or less important than the other members of the team.

Satan uses *jealousy* to destroy on the spiritual realm also. To be envious of the successes of others is an option open even to Christians. God wants all his children to be loyal to him above all. That precludes an overestimation of our personal importance in God's kingdom. The one who provokes the jealousy and the one who is jealous are both thinking of themselves. Joshua 24:19 told the people that God was jealous of their love and loyalty to him. God desires the best for us, therefore, he wants a heart open and ready to receive from him. Godly *jealousy* is for our good. Paul wrote, "For I am jealous over you with godly jealousy: for I have espoused you to one husband, that I may present *you* as a chaste virgin to Christ" (2 Cor. 11:2).

Prayer
Dear God, I want to be a team man, not only for my teammates, but also for you, Lord. Make me a helper and an encourager. Deliver me from jealousy toward the attainments of others.

21.
Judge

. . . behold, the judge standeth before the door.
—James 5:9

He stands with eyes fixed! Any slight movement before the ball is snapped and his flag goes up in the air. The back *judge* has detected an infraction in the execution of the backfield as a play developed. His obsession with the members of the offensive backfield seems almost unfair. Yet there he stands on every play.

The athlete is often the victim of the judgment of an official. Very little gets by the eye of the *judge*, though you may feel his eye is always on you. Games must be played within the framework of rules and regulations, or there would be no just and legal victor. The official has been appointed to see that the game is played accordingly.

Every athlete will tell you that at one time or another he's been beaten by the rules or an interpretation of them. Often it's easier to blame the rules or the officials than to accept our own misconduct. At certain points in a contest, rules can be an advantage. Yet it can always be said that at the moment a rule is favoring you, it is a disadvantage to your opponent.

Judges and officials in this life are but a reminder of an all-seeing *judge* who "neither slumbers nor sleeps" (Ps.

121:4). Regardless of what philosophy you may choose to live by, there are principles which regulate this life. Though he has men to preach and teach his word, God is the final authority. He is always fair and righteous.

As in athletic contests which are regulated by rules, our lives must finally compare favorably with God's word of instruction to us. We are commanded to be "doers of the Word and not hearers only." Every word from God is intended by him to be implemented into our game of life. "He that rejecteth me, and receiveth not my words, hath one that judgeth him: the word that I have spoken, the same shall judge him in the last day" (John 12:48).

Prayer
Master, show me today through the red-flag experiences of life where I need improvement and correction. I submit to you as my righteous judge.

22.

Key

And I will give unto thee the keys of the kingdom of heaven. . . .

—Matthew 16:19

One of the fine points of the game of football is learning to properly read the keys. On both offense and defense, players must learn to *key* on certain positions or maneuvers. The quarterback, in selecting a running play or a pass pattern, is often doing so with an option depending on the reaction of the defense. Practically every defensive player has an option to exercise depending upon what the offensive player opposite him does. Often linebackers and defensive backs are keying on the quarterback or another member of the offensive backfield. I suppose in simple terms, we could say that players do as they do because of what other players are doing. Their reaction is a response to what someone else does.

Isn't that often the way life is? Dr. Otis Strickland says that most of our spiritual problems are confined to temperament, that is, how we react to certain situations. A great deal of our behavior comes from keying on other people. Many of our attitudes about life have been formed by a reaction to a person or situation. All too often we find ourselves generalizing because of a few isolated instances. Some people are

61

not interested in becoming Christians because they have been keying on some phonies. To them, all churches are cold and meaningless because that's the only kind they've ever seen. A few difficult passages in the Bible do not mean it's all vague and impossible to understand. We really need not be reactionaries in all situations of life.

In Hebrews 12:2, we are told to look "unto Jesus the author and finisher of our faith." Jesus is the *key* to life. What a blessed resource in life to be able to interpret everything in the light of a personal relationship to him! Rather than looking at people and responding, God wants us to *key* on his Word and his son Jesus. In the Book of Revelation, recorded by the Apostle John, Jesus said, "I am he that liveth, and was dead; and, behold, I am alive for evermore, Amen; and have the keys of hell and of death" (Rev. 1:18). *Key* on Jesus!

Prayer
Living Savior, I commit my life and all of its experiences to you. May I live keying on you in every situation.

23.

Lame

Then shall the lame man leap as an hart. . . .

—Isaiah 35:6

The "walking wounded" is an endearing group on any athletic team. The team trainer looks over his injury list daily to follow the progress of those who've come up *lame* but hope to soon be back in action. The number on the list may vary, but it usually contains two or three whose absence is sorely felt by the team. Because of the excellent work of our trainers, there is seldom an injury which results in a player becoming *lame* for life. Often because of a player's determination, coupled with the proper care, the trainer can have a player back on the field before the game is over or within just a few hours of his injury.

It is tragic but true that all injuries cannot be remedied with such efficient dispatch. Often injuries become a drama of the pain of the player, the loss to the team, the disappointment to the coaches, and the concern of loved ones and fans.

People in life are often labeled *lame* for various reasons. Sometimes a player who is not thinking sharply is termed a *"lame* brain." A person can go through life nursing hurt or disappointment, thereby carrying with him a lame spirit. In Jesus' day on earth, word soon got around of how he was

63

changing lives in many ways. Those who were defeated and cast down were given new hope through Jesus. Those who were bereaved at the loss of a loved one watched and rejoiced as life was restored. People with withered limbs, bent bodies, blind eyes, and various infirmities from birth were all brought to the Savior for healing. Not only were the *lame* healed, but they leaped and shouted and ran as a result of the Master's touch.

Whether you are *lame* in body or in spirit, Jesus specializes in restoration. A big, strong, healthy body and a *lame*, wounded spirit do not fit together in God's plan for your life. "There came also a multitude out of the cities round about unto Jerusalem, bringing sick folks, and them which were vexed with unclean spirits: and they were healed every one" (Acts 5:16).

Prayer
Great Physician, I bring before you today all my infirmities of body and spirit. I pray the release of your great power that each may be restored in you.

24.
Mark

Brethren, be followers together of me, and mark them which walk so.

—Philippians 3:17

"Watch number 35," says the play-by-play announcer, "He is a young man *mark*ed for stardom." Men who are involved in reporting and developing great athletes are usually quite accurate in predicting the future of players. The progress of such an outstanding prospect is followed closely. The star soon develops into one of whom an outstanding performance is expected every time he takes the field. Those who started out being *mark*ed for stardom are now *mark*ed with great expectation in every game. They are also *mark*ed by the opposing teams as players who must be contained in order to limit their productivity in the game.

The player who is *mark*ed is often an advantage as a decoy. While the opposition is concentrating on the star, other offensive tactics may be used with great effectiveness. Counter-adjustments may only serve to free the star to perform effectively.

In the New Testament, there was a group of people who were *mark*ed. In a city called Antioch, followers of Jesus were first called Christians. They were designated thus be-

65

cause of their similarity and devotion to Jesus Christ. Around the time that Jesus was arrested and eventually brought to trial and crucifixion, a lot of people were being asked, "Are you one of them?" and "Aren't you one of his followers?" Some of Jesus' closest companions denied him in answering this question. They later regrouped under God's power and became a great force for spreading the gospel.

According to God's eternal purpose, all of us who are his children have been *mark*ed to fulfill a specific purpose. Christ has saved us to be a channel of his love and message to this world.

Are you living up to what you have been *marked* to do? Wear the name—and play your game—for his purpose!

Prayer
Father, perhaps today you've marked me for special work in your kingdom. If so, fill me with your divine power as I willingly accept your call.

14. Gap

25.

Miracle

. . . and he hoped to have seen some miracle done by him.
—Luke 23:8

It seems as though every season has its *miracle* team or games which have a miracle finish. The New York Mets once came from last place the year before to win the World Series. The "amazing Mets" they were called. After fifty years without a championship, the 1974 Baylor team won the Southwest Conference football championship and a bid to the Cotton Bowl. Every sports fan would have his own account of a *miracle* finish he himself had witnessed. Many fans came to watch their team knowing full well it would take a *miracle* for them to win this one.

Multitudes followed Jesus throughout his New Testament journeys. A few were devoted and committed disciples, but most were simply waiting to see another *miracle;* a blind man receiving sight or a lame man healed. Though these multitudes were happy to share the benefits of Jesus' miracles, he was primarily a diversion or spectacle to them.

It is one thing to observe Jesus as the *miracle* worker, but quite another to commit your life to him as Savior and Lord. I'm afraid that during the recent so-called "Jesus Movement," our Lord garnered a number of new fans, but not many disciples. Admiring a person for what he is does not bring deep enduring love. Real love and devotion come from loving a person for who he is. The question is "Who is Jesus to you?" Are you just a fan of Jesus, or are you his personal property?

The real *miracle* of the new birth comes when Christ gets behind the wheel of our lives. He then becomes our personal guide and counsel, and under his *miracle*-working power, great things are wrought through our lives.

In Christ, we are destined for the greatest of all *miracle* finishes—the return of our personal Lord and Savior, Jesus Christ.

Prayer
Lord, remind me again today of your great miracle-working capabilities so that seemingly impossible situations become your opportunity. "Into thy hands, O Lord . . ."

26.

Natural

But the natural man receiveth not the things of the spirit of God: for they are foolishness unto him. . . .

—1 Corinthians 2:14

It's the player who has the greatest amount of *natural* ability who raises the highest hopes among coaches and fans. *Natural* athletes are a challenge to any coach to develop and utilize their abilities to the greatest potential. To describe an athlete as *natural* is to say he has certain inborn traits, talents, and reactions which better equip him to excel in sports. This *natural* endowment gives him the potential of excelling in almost any sport he chooses.

One of the great tragedies of sports is to see one with this type of ability become lazy or self-sufficient. To see this kind of ability squandered by a bad attitude or negligence is sad indeed. But what a joy to observe the application of such ability for the betterment of a person's life and the good of the team as a whole.

On the opposite side of the coin, to be *natural* in the spiritual realm is man's greatest downfall. The Apostle Paul taught us in 1 Corinthians 15:50 that "flesh and blood cannot inherit the kingdom of God." Why? Because our flesh has been corrupted by sin. None of us had to learn to do wrong or to think selfish thoughts. We do that quite naturally! In that condition, according to Scripture, we are not in a position to receive the things of God. In fact, we have a *natural* tendency to think of them as foolish. 1 Corinthians 2:14 tells us "neither can he [the natural man] know them [spiritual things], because they are spiritually discerned." In our *natural* state we don't know God; we don't want to know God, and we can't know God! To be described as *natural* in God's eyes is to be lost, unsaved, and with no hope for eternal life.

What must the *natural* man do? He must be raised out of the *natural* and get on spiritual terms with God. This is done by accepting God's son, Jesus Christ, as the sacrifice for sin and as Lord of life. "But as many as received him, to them gave he power to become the sons of God, even to them that believe on his name" (John 1:12).

Prayer
Dear God, thank you for sending the super-natural Jesus that natural men, such as we, might be redeemed.

27.

Net

Let the wicked fall into their own nets. . . .

—Psalm 141:10

To those who play basketball, hockey, tennis, or volleyball, the *net* is a formidable object to be reckoned with. The basketballer loves to hear the swish of the *net* as his fifteen-foot jumper sails through the hoop. The hockey goalie guards the *net* as though it were his very life while the offensive players maneuver for ways to slap the puck in.

In many team sports, as well as fishing, our success depends upon how well we use the *net*. In Bible times the *net* was used as a means to ensnare fish and also animals. Illustrations of the *net* were often used in describing a gathering together.

Tennis and volleyball players can become well known for their outstanding offensive and defensive play along the *net*.

The *net* gives the impression of a rather restricted area. The serves and volleys of a tennis player must have enough elevation to clear the top of the *net*. Regardless of how close the field goal attempt may come, it must slither down through the *net* before it counts.

Jesus talked quite often with men who were accustomed to using nets. Many of his disciples were fishermen, and their catches were of great importance to their livelihoods. When Jesus called them he said, "Come ye after me, and I will make you to become fishers of men." The Gospel of Mark goes on to record, "And straightway they forsook their nets, and followed him" (Mark 1:18).

Whatever your sport, there must be time spent away from your nets in order to become in Christ. There are no Scriptures printed on the covers of basketballs, tennis balls, volleyballs, or any other kind of ball (not a bad idea, though). If you're going to know about God, you must spend time in the Word. Time spent in the Word in fellowship with the Lord will make time spent with the nets all the more productive and enjoyable.

Jesus even has good advice about how to use our nets. Spend time in consultation with him and then say as Peter did, ". . . at thy word, I will let down the net" (Luke 5:5).

Prayer
Loving Father, speak your wisdom to me today. Use me to release those caught in Satan's snare into the net of God's sovereign grace and salvation.

28.

Offer

So Christ was once offered to bear the sins of many. . . .
—Hebrews 9:28

I remember the summer before I began my college education. I had my heart set on where I wanted to go to college, but so far, they had not made me an *offer*. My high school coach had been gracious enough to make a few contacts for me at other schools. He had even taken a teammate and me out to a big league try-out camp where we both did quite well. I was not to be content until the night before I was to go with my high school coach to visit another campus. I was at my girlfriend's house on Sunday night after church. The phone rang, and the *offer* I had been hoping for came through. The recruiter said, "We'd like you to play for us, and we'll pay your tuition and buy your books—plus you can earn spending money with campus jobs." What a relief! I accepted and with great anticipation, I looked forward to the next four years. This experience is multiplied hundreds of times each year as recruiters and athletes discuss offers. It was quite a relief to my parents to know that someone had offered to pay for my college education. It was an *offer* that satisfied all concerned.

Jesus Christ made an *offer* that tops all others. Our sin was to have kept us from knowing God and having a home in eternity in heaven. No lesser sacrifice would have been worthy, nor would it have paid the full price for our sin. Imagine, one *offer* that would take care of the sins of everyone for all time! One sacrifice so worthy as to please God for my sins and yours forever! The Bible says, "For he hath made him to be sin for us, who knew no sin; that we might be made the righteousness of God in him" (2 Cor. 5:21). I see only one sensible choice for man. It's either pay for our own sins in hell, or let Jesus pay for them and live in heaven with him.

I knew where I wanted to go to college. When the *offer* came, the decision had already been made. I simply accepted the *offer*. Christ offers you eternal life if you accept him! Can you make a better choice?

Prayer
Heavenly Father, thank you for your offer of salvation to man. I give you myself today that others may accept your offer of eternal life in Christ.

29.

Oppose

In meekness instructing those that oppose themselves. . . .
—2 Timothy 2:25

Life is filled with opposition. That is why athletic competition contributes to our development. Competition occurs when two teams *oppose* each other. Each is trying to score. Each is trying to win. In facing and responding to opposition, we actually learn some of the cycles of life. We don't always win; we don't always lose, but we are always opposed.

The other team or person is matched against us to provide opposition. Our opponent may be strong, skilled, and quite challenging. There may not be many ways to defeat him. But there is always a way! Persistence and resourcefulness will eventually reveal a chink in the armor someplace.

It is assumed that our opposition comes from our opponent. However, there are times when we *oppose* ourselves, as our Scripture today states. Defeated teams or persons are often heard to say, "We beat ourselves." This is a tragic situation. Your opponent didn't beat you. You were not inferior in ability. You just gave the game away. You opposed yourself.

It is true that man is his own worst enemy. We have a nature controlled by natural and conditioned appetites and ego. 1 John 2:16 describes it as "the lust of the flesh, and the lust of the eyes, and the pride of life." A person acting continually under these influences is more like an animal. (Actually the instinct of an animal will tell it more about what's good for it than a man doing what feels good or "what comes naturally.")

When a team has an opportunity to win and muffs it, there is an indescribable feeling of disappointment. "We had a chance, and we blew it." Through Christ, man has a chance to rise above himself—to be more than a man. Through Christ we can be redeemed, given a new nature and controlled by Christ living within us. While you're making decisions now that will determine future activity, don't limit yourself. The Christ-life is offered to you.

To disregard Christ is a decision in opposition to yourself.

Prayer
God, amidst all of life's opposition today, I give myself to you through your son, Jesus Christ, that I might not continually oppose myself. Lead me in decisions that strengthen me and glorify your son.

30.
Pain

. . . neither shall there be any more pain: for the former things are passed away.

—Revelation 21:4

Nothing can be more discouraging to an athlete than a nagging injury. To play with *pain* is often a greater challenge than meeting and defeating an opponent. *Pain* often indicates a serious injury that can keep a player from practice and participation in a game. Reaction to *pain* can also determine the degree of enthusiasm with which an athlete may play.

The avoidance of *pain* is quite natural to our behavior. It's all in what we prepare for and get accustomed to. A 250-pound tackle who takes and dishes out lick after lick may come near to fainting at the sight of a nurse's needle, or the man who jumps rows of cars on a motorcycle may shy away from riding a bull in a rodeo. The thought of enduring *pain* would always seem to be in the mind of the quarterback as he stands coolly to pass as tons of humanity are bearing down on him.

The player who has been out of action for a time because of injury is encouraged as the *pain* begins to leave his injured limb with each day's workout. In this instance, one must be willing to endure the *pain* of conditioning to relieve the pain of injury.

I believe we can safely say that *pain* is a fact of life. As I heard a coach say once, "You are either in pain now or you're going to be." In Matthew 13:21, Jesus spoke of a type of reaction to *pain*. This person without "roots in himself" can only endure a short time. "Tribulation or persecution" eventually causes him to be offended (discouraged), and he becomes a dropout. Jesus also said, "In the world ye shall have tribulation: but be of good cheer; I have overcome the world" (John 16:33). There is a time coming when God shall wipe away "all symptoms of pain . . . tears from their eyes, no more death, neither sorrow, nor crying." That's when we'll be with Jesus in eternity. But that day will not come without much *pain* and heartache here. Have you prepared yourself?

Prayer
Lord, lead me to face pain and grow stronger in faith that Christ may gain honor through my life.

31.

Prove

Prove me now herewith, saith the Lord.

—Malachi 3:10

Every year, along about September, there are a lot of new things that show up. We have a new school year. The new models of the cars are coming out. There's just a feeling of newness, of starting all over again. This is the time when a lot of things are not yet proven. Though new, they don't yet have the quality of being proven. In the dictionary, the definition of *prove* is "to establish as true, to make certain, to establish the genuineness or validity of." One of the new things that will come out this year will be the new team at school. This is the team that will represent the school. You will be a member of that team. You'll be a part of something that has not been proven yet. To *prove* something is not just to try it out. When we think of trying something it usually implies that you can throw it away if it doesn't work. But you are a member of the team that will be our team all year. If you don't win a game, you will still be the team that represents your school. There are some people who don't like to be proven. They want to walk around acting. I'm a real stud because I act like one. (I also drive a hot car.) You never see a phony in a proving time! Actually, it's quite a compliment to have to go out and *prove* yourself. For instance, this year's team, just by taking the field, really hasn't proven anything, yet. All you have proven is that you know how to put on a uniform and that you know how to come to practice. But that first game, or those first few games of the season, are the real proving times for the team.

There is someone in Scripture that says, "Prove me." His name is Jesus Christ. He was not afraid to be proven. God told people outright in the Scriptures, Malachi 3:10, "Prove me now herewith, saith the Lord." God, in person, said that. Paul, the Apostle, says in Philippians 4:13, "I can do all things through Christ which strengtheneth me." Then in 2 Corinthians 2:14, "Now thanks be unto God, which always causeth us to triumph in Christ." Jesus Christ wants to be proven. He wants you to *prove* him in your life. Just like that new team that takes the field this week or next, for the very first time. All of that practice time, all that energy you have expended, and all the conditioning which you have put into your body are going to be proven. The effectiveness of all of that will *prove* if you are the right kind of competitor and athlete. You should welcome the opportunity to *prove* yourself out on the field. Jesus Christ welcomes the opportunity to prove himself in your life. He is not afraid of what your reaction and your response might be, for Jesus knows that if he has the opportunity to enter your life and become Lord and Master of your life, then all the claims he makes about himself—all that he says that he is and all that he says he can do—he will *prove* in your life if given the chance to do so. Have you proven Jesus in your own life?

Prayer
Lord, I begin this day confident that once again you will prove your power and sufficiency in each experience of life.

32.

Quit

. . . then we will be quit of thine oath which thou hast made us to swear.

—Joshua 2:20

A quitter is one of the least admired personalities of our society. To *quit* is simply to give up, when related to sports. In realms other than sports, *quit* has a more respectable meaning. It means to stop or cease doing. In athletics, "quitter" may refer to a single individual or to a whole team. It may describe a consistent pattern of behavior, or it may involve a single act or response of a person. In any case, to *quit* is an unbecoming trait when related to sports. Yet, often the greatest of athletes entertain the thought. It may never culminate in an action, but in unfulfilling moments, quitting is an option often considered. On an individual basis, quitting is actually a breach of contract with yourself. You're giving up on yourself. In this instance, it is good to remember that after the greatest victories follow the greatest moments of unfulfillment.

A quitter may also be one who is dressed out in full uniform. He may be a performer in the thick of the contest, while in his mind and heart, the game is already lost. It is said admirably of losing teams and players, "They never *quit*" or "They never gave up."

Oftentimes we're tempted to *quit* in the Christian life. The Apostle Paul wrote, "Be ye stedfast, unmoveable, always abounding in the work of the Lord, forasmuch as ye know that your labor is not in vain in the Lord" (1 Cor. 15: 58). Jesus, speaking to John in the Revelation, said, "To him that overcometh will I grant to sit with me in my throne, even as I also overcame, and am set down with my Father in his throne" (Rev. 3:21). Don't be a quitter!

Prayer
God, forgive me for the times I've wanted to quit. In your strength continue to pick me up and thrust me into new challenges for the praise of your son.

33. Running Smooth

33.

Running Smooth

. . . let us run with patience the race that is set before us.
—Hebrews 12:1

The runners are in their starting positions and the gun goes off. 60, 100 or 220 yards later the race is over. As the spectators watch, they marvel at how smoothly the runners move. The effort that surely is required is obscured by the form with which the distances are eaten up. Actually, today's race was a test of how well the runners had been trained. The people in the bleachers hadn't seen the training, the hours of sweat and endurance, the sacrifice that had contributed to the form and smoothness. *Running smooth* comes at quite a price.

Once in a while we run across a person who seems to be *running smooth* through life. Everything seems to be under control. The despair that seems to characterize many is hurdled by the one whom we've observed. But underneath, as with the runner, there's been the patience, training, and endurance to keep eyes focused on the finish up ahead.

Jesus Christ, who began our race of faith, is also the finisher. Some people who haven't begun the race with Christ are going to find the finish to be quite a letdown.

Prayer

Father in heaven, as I enter life's race today, fill me with your patience that others may observe the smoothness of the Christ-life as I run.

34.
Slow

. . . O fools, and slow of heart to believe. . . .

—Luke 24:25

In today's athletic age, to be *slow* is generally to be considered inadequate. No matter how many other plus factors a player may have, if he's *slow,* his lack of reactions or speed of foot prohibit him from competing. Players who are still early in their careers ought to consult coaches and trainers for ways to improve speed and reactions. With all of the advancement in drills and techniques, an athlete can overcome much of his lack of speed and quickness. Of course, for some it may take a great deal more work and application than for others. It all pays off in the long run for a player who expects to have several fruitful years of competition. To overcome a tendency to be *slow* in athletics is paralleled in the spiritual realm. In Luke 24:25, Jesus spoke with directness toward those who were "*slow* of heart to believe." There are those of us who can become quite lazy when it comes to grasping and acting upon truth from the Bible. God has given us the great resource of his Word. He has also given us churches, leaders, teachers, and many other helps toward understanding and appropriating his Word. As with the *slow* athlete, there are some who just naturally have more to overcome in understanding Scripture. Yet it need not remain so. Extra study, prayer, and exposure to God's Word can aid in overcoming our tendency to be *"slow* to believe." This phrase Jesus used can also mean just simply a stubborn refusal on our part. We read. We understand. But we just fail to act on it. To have divine information and direction with no commitment is described by Jesus as foolish behavior.

We must go back to our Bibles. We must ask God to open our minds and refuse Satan the privilege of distracting us. God's teacher, the Holy Spirit, will instruct us if we'll seek his counsel.

"If any of you lack wisdom, let him ask of God, that giveth to all men liberally, and upbraideth [rebuketh] not; and it shall be given him" (James 1:5).

Prayer
Master Teacher, I come into your presence asking you to instruct me in your way. By your power, overcome my slowness of heart.

35.
Sought

And I sought for a man among them. . . .

—Ezekiel 22:30

The days during and immediately following an athlete's
final high school season are both rewarding and frustrating.
If he has performed well, he becomes *sought* after by many
colleges and universities. If the athlete has attained all-star
or blue chip status, he can pick almost any school in the
United States in which to play ball and continue his education. To be *sought* by scouts and coaches means numerous
letters, phone calls, and other contacts at all hours of the day
and night. It can be said that recruiting has now become the
key to the success of any intercollegiate athletic team. Most
coaches will tell you that getting that prospective athlete to
consent and sign to play for them is the hardest thing about
their job. Recruiting is extremely competitive, yet it is a
must.

Just the thought of being sought by someone is a great
reward within itself. It is still a surprise to some athletes
that anyone would want them that badly. Too often it goes
unnoticed that God is on a recruiting program. God is also
seeking young men. In Luke, chapter nineteen, verse ten,
the Gospel writer indicates Jesus came "to seek and to save

91

that which was lost." To be *sought* after and found by God is to be the object of the greatest recruiting program ever known to man. "For God so loved the world, that he gave his only begotten Son, that whosoever believeth in him should not perish, but have everlasting life" (John 3:16). However, to be the object of God's search doesn't depend on your past performance. As 1 Samuel 13:14 says, "The Lord hath sought him a man after his own heart . . . to be captain over his people." While you're being sought by others, don't forget that God is seeking you also. Be found in him and he'll lead you in all your future decisions.

Prayer
Father, I realize to be sought after by God is to be the object of the greatest desire and concern known to man. Thank you Lord!

36.

Speed

. . . let it be done with speed. . . .

—Ezra 6:12

Time is of ever-increasing value. With all the modern innovations that are to free us, it seems we have simply gotten more involved with things that consume our time. We've never had more products which are sold under the *instant* label. Athletic records which seemed unbeatable a generation ago are now shattering right and left. Anything we can learn how to do quicker is purported to be an advancement.

I can remember when it was accepted in sports that the bigger a player, the slower his reactions, particularly in a foot race. If you wanted any speed in your execution, you just had to use smaller, quicker players. But nowadays, linemen outrun the backs quite often in wind sprints. Most pro-linemen must run 40 yards in less than five seconds to be considered adequate. *Speed* is becoming more and more a characteristic of what we do.

God has never been one to waste time either. Though not readily apparent to us, everything God does is done with *speed* and dispatch. It all happens just according to his schedule. God has placed bodies in our universe that move

93

with breakneck *speed,* each timed and right on schedule with the others.

God says he moves to meet the needs of his children. In Jeremiah 33:3 he says, "Call unto me, and I will answer thee, and shew thee great and mighty things, which thou knowest not." In Psalm forty-six, verse five, the Scripture says, "God shall help her, and that right early." God has always been concerned about the conservation of time. The Lord spoke through the Apostle Paul in Ephesians 5:16 and Colossians 4:5 to admonish us to "redeem the time."

Is God getting the most of your time? Some people who can move rather swiftly in an athletic contest slow down considerably in response to God's call. Let it be done with *speed.*

Prayer
I've heard your call, dear Lord. As you always hasten to my need, I come in prompt response to your command.

94

37.
Spring

And they arose early: and it came to pass about the spring of the day. . . .

—1 Samuel 9:26

To a person who enjoys the changing seasons, *spring* is a welcome event each year. From nature's standpoint, *spring* is a time of renewal when flowers and foliage are reborn. All the beautiful things that occur in *spring* are carried over through the summer and autumn until winter comes again.

A welcome sound to an athlete in spring may be the cracking of the bat and the popping of the glove. In most places baseball has its rebirth in springtime. To the footballer, *spring* is an interlude between seasons. There's no league schedule to play, no championship to claim, but hours of long practice and emphasis on fundamentals. *Spring* may also be the time when the outdoor track is again filled with runners prancing like ponies in the fresh, crisp air.

Kurt Kaiser has written a song that says, "Lord, to my heart bring back the springtime. Take away the cold and dark of sin." There are those today who need a springlike renewal inside their lives. The thought of Christ to them just brings a twinge to their heart. They remember times when life was more in Christ than at present. Just as God brings new life

95

through the changing seasons, he desires to draw us back into fellowship with himself. In *spring,* some of the beauty we see comes from seeds and roots of previous plantings. You who've been planted in Christ, he wants to renew that power and peace again within you. But there are also plants and flowers which appear in the *spring* for the first time. These, having sprung from new seed, add to the beauty and freshness of God's world during this glorious season. Some people today, instead of a rebirth, need a new birth. Jesus once told a prominent citizen named Nicodemus, "Ye must be born again." The new birth comes when we open our lives to Christ and God's control. Paul said in 2 Corinthians 5:17, "Therefore, if any man be in Christ, he is a new creature . . . all things become new." *Spring* is here! What comes to mind as you consider your life?

Prayer
Loving Savior, I ask for a newness in my relationship to you. Reveal by the Holy Spirit the inner needs of my heart and bring me to a fresh commitment to Thee.

38.

Staff

Thy rod and thy staff, they comfort me.

—Psalms 23:4

The word *staff*, when used in reference to people and persons, symbolizes support, service, or leadership. In the Bible a *staff* was a rod symbolizing the occupation in which it was used. A person carrying it had the responsibility of caring for and protecting the other people.

Athletic teams are accustomed to the word *staff*. The coaches, whose oversight and responsibility is to lead and mold the team, are known as a coaching *staff*. The work of the *staff* on an athletic team is a source of confidence to the players and the fans. A great deal of dependence is exerted toward any *staff* of coaches by those who work in any phase of the team's development.

The shepherd's assurance of the leadership of his Lord is expressed in the famous psalm from which we've quoted today. There is no leadership that exceeds that of Jesus Christ in our lives; we can be fully confident in him. He knows our opponent; he knows our strengths and weaknesses; he knows the winning game-plan for the game of life.

Christ's *staff* is a symbol of everything we need: leadership, strength, confidence, counsel, instruction, preparation, and conquest. Coaches and players who find their resources in Christ can fully realize and demonstrate the meaning of the *staff*.

Prayer
Lord, I lean on your staff today, realizing that you are the great shepherd of all mankind.

39.

Stand

Watch ye, stand fast in the faith, quit you [conduct your-selves] like men, be strong.

—1 Corinthians 16:13

You can tell a lot about people by watching them *stand*. Posture, facial expression, position of the hips, and balance indicate something about each of us as we *stand*. Watch an athletic contest. You will notice that players at different positions *stand* in different ways. Each position requires its own posture for readiness. My coaches always told me to pay close attention to the stance of each batter. His stance was a clue to how to pitch to him or where he might eventually hit the ball. In the case of a relay team in track, the stance determines how well each runner will receive the baton from the other.

The way we *stand* reveals many things about us. A person who *stands* stoop-shouldered often does so because he/she thinks of himself/herself as too tall. Others may *stand* with head down for fear of looking people in the eye. Some *stand* with a hip to one side because it's "cool" or improves the figure to do so. Standing with the elbows slightly bent outward makes us look bigger and tougher than we are.

It seems people expect a Christian to *stand* differently. The

99

Bible has a lot to say about standing. There are times when we must *stand* with, and sometimes when we must *stand* against. There are very few times when we are privileged to remain neutral as Christians because God has put us here to take a *stand*.

God wants you to be consistent, to *"stand* fast," or firm, as the Word clearly indicates. In Ephesians six, the Bible tells us of armor provided by God which helps us to *stand*. God wants us to trust in his provision. Ephesians 6:13 is a great concluding remark—when we've taken all he provides (the whole armor)—"having done all, to *stand.*" Head up! Shoulders back! *Stand!*

Prayer
It's true, Lord! There are times when I'm tempted to act ashamed when confronted about my relationship with you. Give me your courage and love that I may stand for you.

40.

Stop

. . . Prepare thy chariot, and get thee down, that the rain stop thee not.

—1 Kings 18:44

Momentum is a very important element in an athletic contest. It's a word that simply means "we're rolling." When a team gets the momentum, there's an air of confidence in their execution that seems to say, "Try and *stop* us now!" As a sequel to that confident march, the team against whom the momentum has turned seems to function in an attitude of desperation. "We've got to *stop* them!" A rally is hard to *stop*, but the team who can make a big play and shut down the opposing team's march can quickly turn a game in their favor. "We stopped them!" Some of the most thrilling plays in athletics are of a defensive nature: a goal-line stand, a blocked shot, a leaping, running, one-handed catch by an outfielder, an interception or punt-return.

Yes, we all have our good days—we've got everything together, and we're enjoying great momentum in the game of life. We ought to lift grateful hearts and praise God for days like that. There are also the other days—nothing is going right! So much of the time our only defense is no defense. Our philosophy in these difficult times is often to just let it run its course. Sometimes man's greatest cop-out is "Everything is going to be all right." Listen man! Do you realize that the end of Satan's course is always in your disadvantage? If he is allowed to have his way, he'll destroy you! He must be stopped during those times when he has the momentum in our lives. What if every defensive team looking square in the face of an opposing team's momentum simply threw up their hands and said, "Let them run their course!" Most people are well aware of the direction their lives are going. If your life is heading in a direction away from God, *stop!* God has provided a way through Jesus for you to turn around. Once you're turned around, Satan still fights, but the battle is God's! "Therefore also now, saith the Lord, turn ye even to me with all your heart . . ." (Joel 2:12).

Prayer
Heavenly Father, I realize today there are some things in my life I've got to stop! I come to you for strength to turn around. As I repent, thank you for forgiveness and cleansing.

41. Strength

41.

Strength

The way of the Lord is strength to the upright . . . .
                                        —Proverbs 10:29

I will never forget meeting Paul Anderson for the first time. Here is a man who has lifted more weight than anyone else in the world. His coat size is sixty, that's five feet around the chest! There is tremendous *strength* in those arms and legs as he drives a big nail through two inches of lumber with his doubled-up fist. Paul Anderson began to talk about his life and faith in Christ; the "world's strongest man" said, "I couldn't live one day without Christ in my life."

What Paul was saying is the gist of our Scripture in Proverbs. *Strength* is derived from numerous sources. Physical stature, conditioning, rest, the proper foods, and concentration on certain areas of development are all basic to the *strength* of the body. The final and decisive element to great physical *strength* comes from within. No matter how strong he is, "as he thinketh in his heart, so is he" (Prov. 23:7). King Solomon was enlarging upon a statement made previously as he wrote these words in Proverbs. If a man is what he thinks and the way of the Lord is *strength*, what does that tell us about how to be strong, regardless of the size and development of our bodies?

Strength is for those who avail themselves of the supply. Go ahead! Work, train, condition, nourish, and develop those physical bodies! But remember, the final ingredient is from within. God's way will finish out and complete in you a life of real *strength*. "The righteous also shall hold on his way, and he that hath clean hands shall be stronger and stronger" (Job 17:9).

Prayer

God, strengthen me today as I go deeper into your way. Thank you for strong bodies, but remind me often that real strength comes from within.

42.

Stumble

The way of the wicked is as darkness: they know not at what they stumble.

—Proverbs 4:19

How embarrassing it is to *stumble!* There you are, a few steps from the finish, out in front of the pack—and you *stumble* and fall. In that moment, you are aware of hundreds of eyes fixed on you. How could you do such a thing? It's almost enough to cause you to never want to run again! What caused it? You begin going over in your mind the possible causes: your stride, your shoes, something on the track, or a possible muscle or tendon that gave way. Nothing seems to give a satisfactory explanation. You just simply and humiliatingly stumbled! To a well-trained, well-coached athlete, stumbling usually comes through overconfidence. Underestimating your opponent and overestimating your own ability usually makes for a dangerous turn of events. "Wherefore let him that thinketh he standeth, take heed lest he fall," wrote Paul, who apparently had some experience at running a race.

Stumbling in the Christian life can come in the same way. Oh, I know there are still many things in life a Christian athlete hasn't been coached on. Yet overconfidence in ourselves can be our biggest problem. In the Book of Proverbs, chapter fourteen, verse fourteen, the wise king said, "The backslider in heart shall be filled with his own ways." Our way can literally become our worst enemy. Psalm 37:5 says, "Commit thy way unto the Lord; trust also in him; and he shall bring it to pass." God allows us to *stumble* once in a while to remind us that his way is best. Don't ever get out of the race because you *stumble*. Get up! Keep running, and he'll take you to victory at the finish.

Prayer
Lord, thank you for the stumbles of life that show us our inadequacies. May I look to you on the occasion of each stumble, only to run again in your strength.

43.

Sustain

Cast thy burden upon the Lord, and he shall sustain thee.
—Psalm 55:22

Anyone who follows the sport of football knows that various approaches have been tried and used successfully in developing winning programs. Emphasis on various offensive and defensive formations, the pass, the run, balance, speed and quickness—all are a part of some coaches' philosophy of winning. One popular approach is ball-control through sustained drives toward and across the goal-line. This theory is predicated on the fact that the team who has the ball most will naturally run more offensive plays and score more points. And, in the process, the opposing team doesn't have the ball very often.

How exciting it is to see a team make that crucial touchdown drive in the waning minutes of the game! It wouldn't have been possible without sustaining the offense and maintaining possession of the ball. To *sustain* is to "continue" or "go on."

What a tremendous thought to know that God maintains possession of his own children. He says, "I will never leave thee, nor forsake thee" (Heb. 13:5). God never fumbles the ball or commits a turn-over that results in the loss of one of his team members. Today's text indicates that the Lord also keeps us going. He sustains us. God provides power and instruction through his Word to keep us moving down the field in the game of life. He sustains us on the way to victory. The Apostle Paul once wrote to young Timothy, "But continue thou in the things which thou has learned . . . ." When a crucial decision lies before us in which it looks as though we could lose possession, we must stop and counsel with the Lord and receive power to *sustain* our drive with Christ toward the end zone.

Prayer
Almighty God, you are my sustainer. Through your Word and through fellowship with you, sustain my growth and development in the game of life.

44.

Sweat

. . . and his sweat was as it were great drops of blood falling down to the ground.

—Luke 22:44

Perspiration was pouring from his forehead and the back of his neck. His uniform was drenched above the waist as the sun's rays bore down on this hot afternoon. The big pitcher looked in for the sign from the catcher and began his wind-up for what could be the last pitch of the game. He'd worked hard through eight and two-thirds innings, and his team had gotten him a couple of runs to work on. "Strike three, that's the ballgame!" yelled the umpire. Suddenly the *sweat* that now soaked his body provided a refreshing coolness as his coach and teammates congratulated him. Earlier the moisture on his brow and hands had seemed a nuisance as he tried to grip the ball firmly for the third-strike pitch.

Jesus Christ was sweating it out in the garden of Gethsemane the night before he was to be apprehended. The anquish of the cross was staring him in the face. He prayed, "Father, if it be possible, let this cup pass from me." Then as though reconsidering his words, he spoke to the Father again. "Nevertheless, not as I will, but as thou wilt." Christ's heart was already breaking. His *sweat* was not the clear liquid that

111

normally oozes from the pores of our skin. Instead it had a crimson hue, "as it were great drops of blood." One more great act of sacrifice and the contest for man's soul would be settled. A few hours later as he hung on a cruel cross, words of triumph rang from his lips, "It is finished!" Jesus would never *sweat* in anquish of a cross again! For the Christian athlete now perspiring can help recall the one who *sweat* for our final victory and his victory over sin and death.

"For me it was in the Garden, He prayed 'Not my will but thine,' He had no tears for his own griefs but sweat drops of blood for mine" (Charles H. Gabriel).

Prayer
Lord, again I bless your name for the sacrifice you paid for my sin. Remind me through the perspiration of the contest how you agonized for me.

45.

Take

. . . hold that fast which thou hast, that no man take thy crown.

—Revelation 3:11

It's the game of the year, every year. The archrivals in neighboring states or cities are competing against each other. All of the fans on both sides are heard to say, "We're gonna *take* 'em." In competitive sports, the victory is always up for grabs. Somebody's going to *take* home a win (except in a tie). No matter how high you're ranked, there's always someone out to *take* you! The teams who wear the crowns (championships) must constantly be defending against those who would *take* their crowns from them. The team that owns the trophy always has the threat of having it taken in any given contest. Though it may seem at times as though one school (or team) is winning all the crowns, things even out pretty well. You can observe the trophy case in most schools and see the indication of numerous attainments. Each has crowns to display on behalf of the teams representing the school. There's a great deal of satisfaction in knowing that you personally had something to do with placing that trophy there.

Crowns play a vital part in our Christian lives. An opponent on the field diverts our attention many times through

113

deception. While we're going for the fake, Satan makes advances in our lives through a weakness we've left open. Satan, our opponent in the Christian life, seeks to involve our minds and bodies in other pursuits, thus depriving us of crowns and rewards. Galatians 6:7 says, "Be not deceived . . ." (Don't get taken by one of Satan's fakes). Luke 23:41 tells us, "We receive the due reward of our deeds." These words were spoken by the penitent thief on the cross. Jesus is quoted earlier in Luke six as saying, "Your reward shall be great." Keep your mind on the game, your eyes in the playbook (God's Word), and your ears open to the voice of the coach. If you do, victory after victory, trophy after trophy will be yours in Christ.

Prayer
To be alert and open to your guidance is my prayer, O God, that Satan may not take from me the joy of life at its fullest.

46.

Talent

*But he that had received one [talent] went and digged in the
earth, and hid his lord's money.*

—Matthew 25:18

Talent is a marvelous inheritance from God. It is not given
to be paraded or displayed. Neither is it intended to be buried
in a hole in the ground to rot and be of no possible good.
Talents do not germinate. A hole is no place for them. What
is God's purpose for *talent?* In the rest of the story in
Matthew twenty-five, the lord of those talents expected that
they be invested to bring dividends. Athletic *talent*, rather
than simply for display, is to be invested for the good of the
whole team or institution represented. An athlete who invests
his *talent* for the team usually ends up realizing personal
returns and gains for himself.

Christian athletes are the best. The more incentive an
athlete has, the better he performs. Christian athletes not only
bring recognition to themselves, the team, and the institution,
but Christ is identified with their every move, on and off the
field of play. Plus, these are dividends that not only last for
the season, but may show someone else the way to everlasting
life. "His lord said unto him, Well done, good and faithful
servant; thou hast been faithful over a few things, I will make

thee ruler over many things: enter thou into the joy of thy lord" (Matt. 25:23).

Prayer
Gracious Lord, I give back to you the talents you've given me. Use them to bring honor to your name.

47.

Think

*. . . if there be any virtue, and if there be any praise, think
on these things.*

—Philippians 4:8

Think! Think! Think! How many times have I heard this
from my coaches over the years. The continued repetition of
that five-letter word usually came just after I had missed an
assignment or had made a bad judgment in practice or in a
game. It is true, though. The guy who can *think* under pressure, when the chips are down, is a real asset to any team.
Sometimes there isn't time to assimilate all the facts, sort
them out, and then make a decision. Most of our quick decisions come through practice or a collection of facts based on
someone else's experience. Sometimes when a coach says,
"You're not thinking," he could be saying, "You're thinking
too much." That is, you have other things on your mind that
are obstructing your concentration. The situation at hand
isn't getting all your attention. Most of us aren't smart enough
to think about several things at once and do a good job in
all of them. Being a Christian requires a lot of thought.
Proverbs 23:7 says, "As he thinketh in his heart, so is he."
We are going to be what we *think!* Our level of proficiency in

athletics is going to be in direct proportion to how we apply our minds and concentrate.

Our spiritual lives are influenced in a similar way. Our opening verse in this study is preceded by a list of things which we are to *think* about. These are thoughts which lift a life. By thinking "on these things," we are opening a channel from the windows of heaven for a blessing to be poured out on us (Mal. 3:10). In Matthew 9:4, when Jesus was speaking to a group of doubters concerning his spiritual power, he said, "Wherefore think ye evil in your hearts?" There's no reason why we cannot spend time thinking about things which result in outward traits that are good. Of course, the ultimate thought, determining the root of all good thinking in us, is, "What think ye of Christ?" (Matt. 22:42). What do you *think?*

Prayer
O God, I realize that thoughts may become actions. Guide my thoughts that they may be pleasing to you while contributing to a rich life on earth.

48.

Toss

He will surely violently turn and toss thee like a ball into a large country.

—Isaiah 22:18

Every fall, winter, spring and summer, millions of balls are tossed around as games are underway and athletes are involved in competition. Tossing the ball indicates the ability to maneuver and to control the direction that it goes; a toss is usually a short throw. Coaches teaching football players how to operate the pitch-out may use the word *toss*. Baseball coaches telling how to function around second base or shortstop on the double play, usually talk in terms of the *toss* to the man who's covering the bag. The pitch-out has to be right there for the back to catch it. The *toss* to the second baseman or the shortstop has to be accurate in carrying out the double play properly.

When God speaks of controlling us or maneuvering us, he doesn't always use the terms of a mighty, powerful act. In today's Scripture we notice that the Lord has power to toss us "like a ball." This figure of speech does not indicate lack of power; it simply reminds us that God is in control of us. Though we exercise our wills here upon this earth, God will eventually determine what directions our lives will go in eternity. The Bible says man was created a living soul; we were created in God's image with a spirit that lasts and lives for eternity. God fully intended that his created beings be under his control. Ephesians 4:14 reads, "That we henceforth be no more children, tossed to and fro, and carried about with every wind of doctrine." The Lord intended for us not to be bounced and tossed from pillar to post by every philosophy that comes along. He intended for us to be to his honor and glory as men observe our lives.

Have you ever looked at a ball being tossed around on the field of play and thought about how this describes the lives of many men? Their lives vacillate from one theology to another. They are never able to cement a philosophy about God in their lives that will settle their longing and hunger. If there is a question today about God in your life, something unanswered about God and your relationship to him, I would encourage you not to be tossed around. Don't stubbornly close your mind to God simply because you cannot arrive at a conclusion about him. I would ask you to open your heart to Jesus Christ and invite him to control, maneuver, and to see that your life is moved according to his will and plan. Then, rather than being tossed around yourself, you will be able to control your situations. You, in turn, will be under the control of the one who has the power and ability to control our lives correctly.

Prayer
Lord, today I fix my heart on you. Standing firm in you, keep my heart from being tossed about in uncertainty.

47. Think

49.

Train

Train up a child in the way he should go: and when he is old, he will not depart from it.

—Proverbs 22:6

A paraphrase of this verse for a coach would be, *"Train up a player in the way he should go, and when he is in a game, he will not depart from it."* Training is a vital part of a successful athlete. Training takes place twenty-four hours a day. It includes the proper diet and the proper amount of rest. The player spends time off the practice field thinking of ways in which he can improve himself. He studies the formation, the system by which his team will be run. When a wrestler is in training, he is constantly aware of what his body is taking in, in order to maintain his playing weight that guarantees maximum response, efficiency, and reaction. Training requires dedication, not only to the game itself, but also to that which makes us more available to respond to what the game requires. Most athletic events and contests require more than just knowledge of the game. They require that we apply ourselves. Sacrifice is involved so that our bodies can be presented in a favorable condition along with all of the knowledge and the practice. Training. An essential, vital part of being a good athlete.

Scripture teaches us to *train*. The verse that we mentioned at the beginning of this study is one that parents have read for years. In teaching and training parents can provide wholesome experiences for their child so that he can be trusted when he is on his own. Athletic training is prescribed to make us available to respond to whatever demands the game makes upon our bodies and minds. You are training not only to participate on the team of which you are a member, but also to be able to participate in life. Every man betrays his background in a crisis; he shows how he has been trained to respond to certain experiences in life. The thing that really identifies any man is his purpose. There are certain ingredients that go into establishing the proper purpose of life. Training to achieve a right purpose of life requires putting things that contribute to high and wholesome standards into our lives and our minds. Having put the proper background and basis upon which to have a high standard of living into our lives, we can enter a more mature level of life.

Having trained to do so, you have resolved in your heart to play the game hard, to play the game honestly, to play it according to the rules, with the best interest of the team in mind. These resolutions will contribute to a high standard of life. Resolve in your heart to put into your mind music, art, and literature that will contribute to a wholesome outlook. Do not lower your standards with so many of today's worldly impurities. David the psalmist said, "Thy Word have I hid in my heart, that I might not sin against thee." The Bible, placed in our hearts through use, memorization, and reading, as well as through hearing the preaching and teaching of it, gives us a basis and a background upon which to build a high standard of life. Training contributes to a worthwhile life— prayer and fellowship with our heavenly father, fellowship and intimate relationships with other people who have a high standard of life, and a faith in Christ. God gives us these avenues to train us up, to render us available to him for the highest of all lives, that of living in fellowship and in the power of Christ. Regardless of the plateau of life into which we move, we should never discount the importance of training. Training continues to be an important element of a life in the power of God—life existing so that men everywhere can be blessed and lifted up through it. A life like this requires our willingness to *train*.

Prayer
I submit myself, O God, to your training program. Guide me each day to develop in a greater commitment and usefulness for you.

50.

Triumph

Now thanks be unto God, which always causeth us to triumph in Christ. . . .

—2 Corinthians 2:14

If you could sit down and draw up a sure plan for winning —a plan, which if operated to proficiency and perfection, would always produce victory—you could distribute, sell, and put that plan into effect anywhere competitive teams meet. How to win? A design for *triumph* is a precious commodity. Every year coaches travel many hundreds of miles to hear other coaches speak and give their philosophies and their systems on how to win. Many things are brought back, applied, and put into effect in athletic programs to see if there is a winning combination. Is this a winning formula? Once in a while, through the evolution of various formations and formulas, there seems to come to the surface one which is successful. I recall when the split-T was practically unbeatable. The offensive lines were split, leaving such a gap between each of the offensive linemen that there was already a hole there even before a block was made. Soon other formations began to replace that. Today we have the wishbone. Successful as it seems, already there are defenses now being contrived which will probably render the wishbone obsolete one day. But in the evolution of formations and formulas, one eventually comes to the surface that has to give in and give sway to another. So, there really isn't one particular formula for winning that has been true and in effect all along.

There are principles that, when applied to the game and adhered to 100 percent, produce the kind of athlete who can win. In 2 Corinthians 2:14, we are given a formula that always produces triumph. Paul was writing, "Thanks be unto God, which always causeth us to triumph." There is a formula for life that guarantees *triumph* and victory in every situation. People are searching for a formula for living, a formula for *triumph*. The only place of assured *triumph* today is in Jesus Christ. It is not in the abilities or talents of men. They can be pitted against the abilities and talents of other men, only to find somewhere down the line, that the abilities and talents of other men measure up. *Triumph* is not found in possessing a high degree of educational training. There have been men who hold high degrees whose lives have been an absolute failure. Education is important, and God uses it to an advantage to those who will submit it to him. The formula for being triumphant in every situation is to be found in Christ. Regardless of what people may say (criticisms and evaluations by people many times who are spokesmen for Satan), the best athlete is still the Christian athlete. The best student is still the Christian student. The best son or daughter is still a Christian son or daughter. We can be thankful that in Christ (that is, in a vital, resting, abiding relationship with him), there is always *triumph*. There is never a loss, regardless of what the scoreboard may show. You can tell a winner by the way he walks off the field. Even though the score may not be in his favor, he still has his head up; he still has his confidence in the proper source. Christ makes winners out of all those who are in him.

I recall one summer going away to a church camp. About

a half-dozen of the finest athletes from our local high school were in our group. Up until that time the school had not been a consistent winner in sports. While we were at camp that summer, those young men learned that Jesus Christ abiding in them was the only sure formula for *triumph.* We competed together in softball against other church groups at camp, many of whom had fine athletes on their teams. Our team came away with victory after victory and eventually with the trophy, but they came away with much more than that. These young men learned how to be winners, learning that in Christ, by planting and placing all of their lives and abilities in God, he would assure them of triumph in every situation. They not only learned how to compete in athletics, but they learned how to live life. They learned how to live in *triumph* over the temptations and onslaught of Satan and all his evil power. There is no other formula that can say, "always causeth us to triumph." To be in Christ is simply to place all that you are, all that you have been, and all that you intend to be into his hand. Allow him to make the decisions and to function, compete, study, and to obey through you. Be available for all of his power in you. Thanks be unto God. That's real and assured *triumph!*

Prayer
Master, teach me to be a winner on my team. As you make a winner of me, use me to impart triumph in Christ to my teammates.

51.

Unity

Behold, how good and how pleasant it is for brethren to dwell together in unity.

—Psalm 133:1

Some of the most pleasant memories that I have from my sports experience is the *unity* that I felt with fellow teammates and coaches. Realizing that as you are taking the field with nine others, or eleven, or five, you all have one common goal of playing together is beautiful, uplifting, and satisfying. It is a noble quest to represent that team and share together in whatever the results of the contest may be. I recall, on a number of occasions, how much joy we shared in a victory—how each felt his own contribution to the victory. I recall on a few occasions how deep the agony was in sharing a defeat together—knowing that no one person had been to blame or at fault. As a team, we had suffered a defeat and a setback together. We knew it had happened as we competed together. The unity of endeavor, the *unity* of spirit, is strong as we approach the challenge of meeting an opponent with our collective abilities and our collective dedication. These are marvelous memories and recollections; they are also some of the greatest advantages of team participation offered to the participant. *Unity.* What a marvelous word!

What a fine experience to look around the locker room and see numbers of your friends wearing the same colors, the same uniform, each representing and giving themselves to the same cause. To be a part of an endeavor like this has encouraged and inspired young men for centuries. Even professional teams, which are perennially accused of playing simply for the financial benefits, will admit to a great deal of satisfaction in being a part of a fellowship, a *unity*, a team.

Unity of purpose is characteristic of the team that wins. The teams that have the greatest degree of *unity*, who can play together, work together, and function smoothly, are the teams who become winners. These are the teams who play with *unity* and are feared the most, though they may not possess great ability or players who individually stand out. Their success does not depend upon the ability and talents of one or two. Their strength is in the *unity* with which they move into the contest, facing the challenge together. In the Book of Psalms King David, leading his armies to battle and seeing the citizens of his community, remarked, "How good it is for brethren to dwell together in unity." King David was speaking of what he had seen in the lives of people with a common cause.

There is no greater common cause known to the world today than the cause of Jesus Christ. Those who endeavor in *unity* for that great cause reveal the greatest testimony that this world can observe—a far greater testimony than the ability of people to teach and to preach God's Word. *Unity* is a far greater testimony of the validity of the Bible and of Jesus Christ than all the tall spires on the tops of churches throughout the world. Paul, in writing to the church of Ephesus, put great emphasis on *unity*. In Ephesians 4:3 he said, "Endeavoring to keep the *unity* of the Spirit in the bond of peace." So many times we let our own opinions become paramount in what we are doing. We want people to hear what we have to say. We want people to do what we suggest, and in the process *unity* is affected. If the team taking the court becomes dominated by various opinions or by the desire of one person to excel above the others, then *unity* becomes affected. If one team member becomes obsessed with his own welfare, the team unity is affected. The Apostle Paul further emphasized *unity* when he said, "Till we all come in the *unity* of the faith and of the knowledge of the Son of God unto a perfect and mature man, unto the measure of the stature of the fullness of Christ." That is what we are moving toward. Spectators would rather see a team operate with *unity* than see all of the individuals. One particular individual is a sight to see, but a team which can take the court and function with *unity* is a greater pleasure to watch.

The world is going to get the most palatable taste of Christianity from Christians who move and operate with *unity*. We need to give ourselves to the cause of Jesus Christ to allow him to create Christian character in us that makes us more concerned with the *unity* of the team than with any other factor involved in the contest.

Prayer
Father, unify our team as we play together, and ever more unify us in the love of Christ that we may play as his representatives.

52.

Unprepared

. . . that, . . . ye may be ready: Lest haply if they . . .
come with me, and find you unprepared. . . .
—2 Corinthians 9:3, 4

Preparation is basic to all areas of life. To enter a contest *unprepared* is to invite situations that we don't know how to cope with. Preparation is for the purpose of rehearsing and practicing situations which may occur in the actual contest. To face a challenge *unprepared,* having had opportunity to rehearse and practice, is inexcusable. What sudden fright comes upon us, as we are in a game situation, to suddenly find a formation or lineup for which we have not prepared! Because of the experience of being *unprepared* and the reaction it creates, most of us would rather have time to prepare. Ample preparation makes us feel somewhat secure in facing various situations. In fact, that's the name of the game. We look forward, from week to week and night to night, to contests where we will be confronted with an opponent. We want to be prepared. We don't like to walk into a classroom knowing there is a test ahead of us without being prepared. We don't like to take on responsibilities without having prepared to do well.

Life requires preparation for us to be able to cope with it.

Amos was a prophet of God who went about the country telling people to prepare to meet God. "Prepare to meet thy God" (Amos 4:12). There's a rather strange paradox in our society. People are conscious of their need to prepare in many areas, yet, when it comes to preparing for God, we feel that God, being a gracious father, looks upon our weaknesses with indifference. The truth of the matter is, God has given us much with which to prepare for him. We must all prepare to stand before him one day. Preparation for that experience can only take place now. Preparation in meeting God also involves preparation that he has made. Jesus said in John 14:2, "I go to prepare a place for you." At this very moment, as you are reading these words, there is preparation going on in heaven for us. Jesus said, "If I go and prepare a place for you, I will come again and receive you unto myself that where I am, ye may be also." He is preparing a place of residence in eternity with him. There are scores of people walking this earth today who never give it a second thought that there is preparation required in meeting God. What a tragedy—to realize that one day God is coming! We will be meeting him, and he has made all the preparation necessary, but we stand *unprepared* to meet him. I pray that as you contemplate these thoughts you will realize that today must begin a preparation time for you to meet God. Preparation to meet God involves inviting Jesus Christ into your heart as the lord and master of your life. He comes by invitation. He says, "Behold, I stand at the door and knock." He will not come in until he is invited. Have you prepared for God by inviting Jesus Christ into your life?

Prayer
Dear God, thank you that in Jesus we make preparation to meet you. In the midst of so many who are unprepared, use me to show the way to you.

53.

Victory

. . . *and this is the victory that overcometh the world, even our faith.*

—1 John 5:4

"Victory, victory is our cry, *V I C T O R Y.* Are we in it, well I guess, Alma mater, yes, yes, yes!" This has been the cry of many cheering sections as their teams were taking the field in combat against another team. *Victory* is the pursuit of every coach and every player. A simple definition of *victory* is that in a game of skill and strategy, your team comes out with the advantage. The winning score is yours as you leave the field and go back to your school with a *victory. Victory* is a very satisfying moment. *Victory* is the culmination of a lot of hours, a lot of application. It is a satisfying feeling, as you well know, to go home realizing that all you have put into this endeavor has resulted in *victory* over your opponents. Some victories are more satisfying than others. A *victory* over an archrival or one under whom you have suffered defeat in some previous occasion is a great satisfaction. Victories over the so-called rated teams, the premier opponents, bring a great deal more satisfaction than victories in games we were supposed to win.

In the game of life all of us have an archrival. He has

been competing for our attention and our energies for most of our conscious existence. His name is Satan, and he operates and functions through the available resources of this world. When the Bible talks about the world, it is indicative of a phrase meaning "world systems." In John's Gospel in chapters twelve, fourteen and sixteen Satan has been designated "the Prince of this world." If you and I are to overcome this world and its prince, it is going to take a *victory*. Many times when a person confronts a powerful opponent, he is satisfied simply to come away with a tie or a draw, with nothing decided. There are people who have come to a point in their lives, at Satan's own suggestion, that they simply co-exist or play him to a stand-off. They win a few, and he wins a few. This is a very satisfying existence for Satan because he exercises his knowledge of us. Because of our nature, we have a tendency to be more like him than like God. He knows us and knows where he can defeat us.

Any person who has been in an athletic contest knows a tie-game is very unsatisfying. No *victory*, no loss. One of Satan's main objectives is to get our lives in a deadlock so that we never know *victory* over him. We may never know how to exercise a *victory* over our opponent Satan. If Satan can get us to concede that he is too powerful, if he can get us to concede that we can't whip him, then he has the game won, and the deadlock will be broken. No team is ever more pathetic than when, after being stymied time and time again, they get the attitude that they can't win. And a team that feels they can't win is a certain loser. Satan wants us to believe that we can't win against him. He would like for us to think that he is too powerful, too knowledgeable, too cunning, and has too much ability for us to be able to compete with him under any circumstance.

This passage that we quoted at the beginning is the *victory*. Faith causes us to believe that we have a coach, a leader, one

135

experienced in the combat with Satan. Jesus met Satan in the wilderness (Luke 4) and overcame him. Jesus overcame him again when he went to the cross because there Jesus provided us with power to live in victory. That word "faith" is mentioned here. Faith enables us to believe that what Jesus did upon the cross in dying for our sins was for us personally, and in that experience, he defeated Satan. "And this is the *victory*, even our faith." John goes on to say in verse five, chapter five, "Who is he that overcometh the world, but he that believeth that Jesus is the Son of God." Do you want to know *victory* in the game of life? Do you want to know *victory* over your archrival, Satan? Open your heart to Jesus Christ and allow him (in you) to be your *victory* over Satan. Give each day to the Lord—each trial, each test, and each encounter with Satan—and God will be your strength. And the reason our *victory* is possible and assured is that "greater is he that is in you, than he that is in the world" (1 John 4:4). When we allow Jesus to control, direct, and fill our lives, then he has the greatness and the *victory* over the one (Satan) who is in the world.

Prayer
Thank you, Lord, for victories on the field of play. Let me not live in defeat in the spiritual realm, but let me realize that Christ is my victory in life each day.

54.

Weakness

My grace is sufficient for thee: for my strength is made perfect in weakness.

—2 Corinthians 12:9

There have been athletic teams down through history who have fielded a lineup which showed no *weakness*. The Miami Dolphins, Super Bowl champions for two consecutive years, is such a team. So were the winning teams of Greenbay and the great New York Yankees, who dominated the World Series in years past. There are those men in professional golf and tennis, who reportedly have no weakness in their consistent, powerful games. But most of us have not had the privilege of playing without a *weakness* or even participating on a team without a *weakness*. In most instances there is a *weakness* that can be found in any team that takes the field to play. In preparing for important games, coaches spend time not only strengthening areas where they are strong, but also bolstering their own weaknesses. They also give careful attention to the weaknesses of the opposing team. There have been games won and lost on the ability of one team to exploit the *weakness* of another team. Many times weaknesses don't begin to show until put under stress. Many teams which have entered a playing field feeling strong begin to show *weakness* under the pressure of a good team. Any athlete who is to improve himself must realize his areas of *weakness* and spend time dedicated to overcoming those weaknesses. Weaknesses can be turned into strengths. Sometimes a team, having won by exploiting the *weakness* of another, will find upon a re-encounter that a former *weakness* has become a strength.

One of the great tragedies of life (and sports) is that some weaknesses are never realized. The beginning step toward remedying a *weakness* and making it a strength is to realize that it exists. There have been teams who have taken the field week after week and have been beaten over and over in the same way. They apparently never realized their *weakness.* There have been individuals who constantly took their responsibility as a team member without realizing that there was a glaring *weakness* in their game or that they needed to apply themselves to that *weakness.* In writing the passage for the text in today's thought, Paul said that there had been a problem in his life. It continued over and over, and had become to him "a thorn in the flesh." "I besought the Lord three times." He went to God in prayer about it. God assured him he would provide strength and grace to meet that *weakness.* God said, "My strength [the strength that I will give you] is made perfect in weakness [in the realization of your *weakness*]." God cannot apply his solution or his power to a *weakness* that we will not admit. We can continue to live with a *weakness* or a fallacy in our lives. In many cases, we can even justify that *weakness* by observing other people's lives. In comparison with other people's lives, a *weakness* doesn't seem too important. But when we realize our own weaknesses and realize that God in his strength and power can overcome these weaknesses in us, what fools we are to continue to live in the *weakness* that besets us. If there is a *weakness* in your game today, you need to apply yourself for the good of the team and for your own good. If there is a *weakness* in your

138

life, if the Holy Spirit lives in you and you are a child of God, then that power living in you will make known to you weaknesses in your life. Bring them before God in confession, then God can turn these weaknesses into strengths. God wants to do this; he delights in it. He tells us in his Word, "If any of you lack wisdom, let him ask of God, that giveth to all men liberally, and upbraideth not . . ." (James 1:5). God wants to give his strength. He wants us to be possessed and filled with his power and not to live continually under defeat and aggravation in our lives. What is your *weakness?* Admit it to God and ask him to apply his power to make it a strength to your life.

Prayer
Lord, today I confess my weakness. I claim your promise that in Christ strength is made perfect in weakness. Thank you, Lord.

59. Wrestle

55.
Weather

When it is evening, ye say, It will be fair weather: for the sky is red. And in the morning, It will be foul weather to day. . . .

—Matthew 16:2, 3

Weather is a real factor in outdoor sports. There are many coaches and players who have walked outside the dressing room a few moments before the game was to begin and looked up into the sky to try to determine what the *weather* was going to be for the game. The *weather* makes a lot of difference in many things—in the condition of the playing field, in the condition of the ball, how it's to be handled and thrown, caught and kicked. Weather makes a difference in the traction determining the way players run and how well the blockers are able to move other bodies out of the way so ball carriers can run. The *weather* has been a serious factor in athletic contests for years. Many times it also determines the playing capability of a ballplayer. We have heard it said, "He is a fair-weather ballplayer." That usually means that not only must the *weather* be bright, sunny, and dry, but, for him to put out and do his best, everything has to be working in his favor. A fair-weather ballplayer is generally one who is evaluated to be consistent only as the elements or situations

143

around him are consistent. He is not known for his ability to overcome or to play above and beyond the difficult circumstances of life. He is usually held out by his coach until certain circumstances are favorable for him to perform according to his ability. On the other hand, *weather* can become an equalizer between teams. A team that is purported to be well coached and ready—a winning team with great ability and precision—can find its ability equalized by an opposing team of less ability according to the condition of the field. So, *weather* is an obvious factor in athletic contests.

Weather is also a factor to be considered in life. There are times in our lives when the *weather* doesn't seem to be favorable, when we have to readjust ourselves as we face a storm. These are the times which test what kind of a ballplayer we are in life. These are the times when we find out if we function well only when all the circumstances seem to be favorable. There are some people who just can't seem to make it under adverse circumstances—circumstances which seem to call for a little extra or require resources that we have not yet used. Jesus allows various types of *weather* in our lives to show us that he is capable of providing the power and resources for all of our needs. There is a recent song that says, "If I never had a problem, I would never know that he could solve them; I would never know what faith in God could do." As a ballplayer can never know what resources it takes for him to meet the challenge of inclimate *weather,* so a person in life who goes along in a fair-weather existence will never know what it is to call upon the deepest resources of God to meet the different kinds of problems and trials that come. A fair-weather ballplayer has let it be known by his ability and by the way he plays in certain conditions that he will not be an asset to the team under difficult times.

A fair-weather person, particularly a fair-weather Christian, has let it be known that his Christianity depends upon favorable conditions. In an attitude like this, he never shows the great resources of God to meet all needs, regardless of the *weather* and circumstances around us. In John 16:33 Jesus spoke these words, "These things I have spoken unto you, that in me ye might have peace. In the world, ye shall have tribulation: but be of good cheer; I have overcome the world." Think of it! Living inside us is one who has overcome these problems. Jesus himself spoke, quieting the storms and the seas. He quieted the *weather*, and that same Jesus living in us shows his power and authority over this world. You and I as Christians need not live our lives looking out the windows, looking up at the sky, trying to see what the *weather* of life is going to be. We need not be fair-weather Christians, but instead we can welcome every type of *weather* that life has to offer as a challenge and opportunity for God to prove himself in us.

Prayer
Lord Jesus, I realize you are the same yesterday, today, and forever. I confess that whatever the climate of my life, you are the consistency for all types of weather.

56.

Weigh

. . . thou, most upright, dost weigh the path of the just.
—Isaiah 26:7

The time when we weigh-in to see how we are complying with the trainer's request for our weight is one of those times we look forward to each year. Some of those big fellows with extra pounds probably look with less anticipation toward this time than others do. When we find out how much we *weigh*, then we can tell how the program's been going. How well have we been complying with our diets, and how well has the weight been coming off? Many times, to the dismay of some players, the weight doesn't come off as it was prescribed to do. This simply means that more hard work and sweat are required. He's got to discipline himself more. Many times men have stepped on the scales with great anticipation, having felt that things were going to be all right, only to find that the scales didn't show that they had lost the right amount of weight. They thought they had worked and sacrificed, doing all that was necessary for the weight to come off. Then they find that more is still being required. So, back to the field, back to the workouts, looking forward to another time to stand on the scale. But, when finally we step on the scale and see that we have made the weight, there are shouts of great

146

glee. The wrestler has to consider weight every day as he works out; a boxer realizes that in order to compete in a certain level of competition, his weight must comply with the level of his class. So for many people, the scale is something they look forward to daily. They have to be careful all the time of how the scales balance when it comes to their weight against the standard.

In this passage in Isaiah, we see that the Lord is in the business of weighing. In the Book of Daniel a great king was told that he was weighed in the balances and found wanting. God is constantly weighing the spiritual life of his children. God is weighing the path which we walk continually; he is concerned that our lives balance out in respect to his direction. He intends our lives to go his way, and he is constantly reminding us through his Holy Spirit that areas of our lives are out of balance. I'm thankful that we have a God who is concerned about our weight. He doesn't want us to gorge ourselves and get all out of balance. There are people who let their lives get out of balance to the point that to get back in fellowship with God (to get back in a favorable weight on the scales of God), they have to go on a crash diet. God has a program to get them back in fellowship and in the proper weight on his scales. The Bible tells us that one of these days the scales will be balanced for the last time. We do not have forever to balance the scales of our lives. Some people are going through life today not really caring what balance their lives have; they don't care that their lives are tipping too far in the direction of Satan and destruction. They are content to gorge themselves on their own wants and desires; they live by the standard of one who intends to destroy and to render their lives ineffective. Yet, God is concerned! God is just and constantly concerned how we balance in this life.

What are the scales going to read when we step on them? Maybe you could take a moment and spend some time in private fellowship and private prayer with God even now as you read. Ask the Lord to reveal the balance of your life, the scale. How much do you *weigh* in God's standard? How much do you *weigh* on the scale of life? Have you gotten to a point where things have gotten way out of balance and kilter? You may need to look into God's crash diet program to get back into fellowship with him. There are many things that help to balance our lives before the Lord—he gives us his word; he gives us the precious truth of that book as we read it; he shows us the directions and applications that our lives must have. There are conversations, fellowship, and prayer that are used by God to balance our lives favorably. Sharing Christ Jesus in a personal witness is an investment of our lives that other people might know life. This balances life. In all that we do in the participation on the field, the court, the mat, or the diamond, God wants to be an outreach that others might know life, his life. This is a staggering thought, but a serious and necessary one for us today—"How much do I *weigh* on God's scale?" What is needed to get back in the proper balance of life as far as God is concerned?

Prayer
Blessed Savior, give me a vision of my life in your balances today. Remind me again that Jesus is the hope of balancing my life and making it acceptable to God.

57.

Winning and Losing

Yea doubtless, and I count all things but loss for the excellency of the knowledge of Christ Jesus my Lord: for whom I have suffered the loss of all things, and do count them but dung, that I may win Christ.

—Philippians 3:8

Winning and losing is the whole philosophy of athletics, or so it seems. A team is a success if they win, a failure if they lose. No team ever took the field for any other reason than to win. The purpose and reason for taking the field, even under the most uncertain circumstances or the highest of odds, was to win the contest. However, any team that takes the field risks the possibility of losing. Some people's attitude is to play it safe—to not get in the contest, to protect their record. By this philosophy they think they will never be a loser. Most people standing on the sidelines, armchair quarterbacks, can look at your actions. They haven't been in the contest, and not having put themselves in the position of winning or losing, they can assess what you did and try to come up with a decision as to what you should have done. These people know it is much easier to stand on the sidelines and call the plays for other people than it is to get in the contest themselves. To get in the contest yourself requires suffering the possibility of

149

being either a winner or loser. As Paul indicated, a team has to suffer the agony of losing on numerous occasions before the winning combination comes. Sometimes a team has to suffer a number of losses in learning what it takes to win. If in the process of losing, they learn their weakness and learn areas that need to be strengthened, then as they continue to work on these areas each week they will improve. It isn't long until they get into the win column. Paul said, "for whom I have suffered the loss of all things."

Here is the characteristic of a winning team. Any team that wins has team members who are willing to lose everything. They play with reckless abandon, with all they have—literally, to lose themselves that the team might win. Paul went on to say, that though I have suffered the loss of all things, the reason is that "I might win Christ." That I might win! What a prize for life! What a prize to possess and be a part of, knowing Jesus Christ as a result of study, sacrifice and loss. So many times those on the sidelines don't understand what the Christian athlete is putting aside in order to be a winner. It means putting aside some of his personal wants and ideas and also putting aside extracurricular things—laying aside those things that aren't good for himself and aren't good for the team either. Yes, it means losing those things in order that he and the team might eventually come out on the winning column. As in an athletic contest, the Christian life requires us to get into the game. We're not to stand on the sidelines and criticize those who are supposed to be Christian. It's a lot easier for people to stand around and evaluate other people's Christian lives than it is to get in the game themselves and offer their lives to Christ. We must all eventually realize that we suffer the loss of ourselves in order to gain the full and complete victory in Jesus Christ. *Winning and losing* in life is directly related to how many hours of our day or how much of our life is under the control of Jesus Christ, our

150

Lord and Savior, our great coach. We will never be what we could be as a student, until Jesus Christ in us is allowed to be that student. We will never be the athlete that we could be until Jesus Christ is allowed to be that athlete in us. Suffering the loss of ourselves. Are you winning or losing?

Prayer
Almighty Father, I want to lose myself today in Jesus. Send me into the game of life and demonstrate your power to win through me.

58.

Work Out

Wherefore, my beloved, as ye have always obeyed . . . work out your own salvation . . .

—Philippians 2:12

The games are great, but the work-outs can be drudgery. In fact, the thing that makes the *work-out* important is that ball game, meet, or match coming up soon. In order for the team to do well, every member of the team will want to *work out* and work hard to the good of the team, because he is a member of the team. (Notice: working out doesn't make you a member of the team.) In writing to the Christians at Philippi, the Apostle Paul encouraged them to work out, to constantly be practicing their faith in Jesus Christ. As with an athletic contest, we play the game of life just about the way we practice it. No team is going to take the field and play consistently better than it has practiced. The contest and challenge of life takes on quite a different look when we've spent time working out our salvation. As with the parenthetical statement above, we don't work out our salvation in order to be saved, we work out because we are saved (having invited Christ into our lives) (Rom. 10:13).

No amount of working out and just hanging around the team will make you a member of the team. You'll never get in the game until you join the team—then you've got a chance to practice, wear the uniform, and get into the game. Then your practice takes on the significance of being a team member looking forward to the game. What a difference! Every day is a *work out* for our life in Christ. What a gracious coach and teacher he is! Yes, Christ teaches us, but he also empowers us to not only *work out*, but in and through and over and around this needy world we live in. "And they went forth, and preached every where, the Lord working with them, and confirming the word with signs following" (Mark 16:20).

Prayer
Lord, today I release myself completely to your life in me so the world may see Christ working out of my life.

59.

Wrestle

For we wrestle not against flesh and blood. . . .
                                        —Ephesians 6:12

An enemy we cannot see is engaging us in a real struggle. If we could just get our hands on him, if he'd just come out in the open, we'd take him down and pin his shoulders to the mat. Satan tries to rule us through the domain of ideas and attitudes. His field of competition is "principalities and powers." He tries to get in as much riding time as possible to keep us under his craftiness. Not all of our combat in life is waged on the mat. It takes real courage to meet a man hand to hand in open competition. But it takes equal courage to stand up to those opponents we cannot see or get our hands on—those opponents that are competing for our heart and our minds. God's Word says, "As he thinketh in his heart, so is he" (Prov. 23:7). To win this match, we must learn to submit our hearts and minds to a power who can *wrestle* and win in the struggle with Satan. If Jesus Christ is in your life, you have immediate, wise, and ready counsel to meet Satan on the mat and keep him under the established dominion of his superior.

When you're wrestling with a problem or when there is a combat going on in your mind, remember the words of Scripture which say, "If any of you lack wisdom, let him ask of

154

God, that giveth to all men liberally, and upbraideth not; and it shall be given him" (James 1:5).

Prayer
Blessed Master, I acknowledge my personal futility in wrestling with my spiritual opponent. Thank you that Satan is already defeated by your power in me.

60.

Your Name

. . . So didst thou get thee a name, as it is this day.
—Nehemiah 9:10

In all team sports there is generally a number which designates each player. He has a number to the officials, the score keeper, and the fans watching the contest. But if you'll look at your line-up closely, you'll notice that every player also has a name. The more prominent a player gets, the more people remember the name that goes along with his number. Most sports fans know who number 32 is for the Buffalo Bills; his name is Simpson. We know who number 44 is for the Atlanta Braves; his name is Henry Aaron. In Old Testament times, people were named for what they were. For instance, Jacob meant "supplanter" or "trickster"; he was slippery. Samson's name meant "like the sun"; he was powerful.

What would it be like if people started calling us what we are? What if we had to be something before we were given a name describing what we are? What would your name be? The disciples were first called Christians at Antioch. It was kind of a tag when it first started, but it stuck. Jesus Christ was given a "name which is above every name." I guess that makes being called Christian quite a privilege. "Nevertheless the foundation of God standeth sure, having this seal, The Lord knoweth them that are his. And, Let every one that nameth the name of Christ depart from iniquity" (2 Tim. 2:19).

Prayer
Lord, I desire to be worthy of the name Christian today as you fill me with your spirit and actually live through me.